AF557829

Aspire to Inspire Revisited

Aspire to Inspire Revisited

Manisha Kanoria Lohia

Published by Ashok Gosain and Ashish Gosain for
HAR-ANAND PUBLICATIONS PVT LTD
E-49/3, Okhla Industrial Area, Phase-II, New Delhi-110020
Tel: 41603490
E-mail: info@haranandbooks.com/haranand@rediffmail.com
Shop online at: www.haranandbooks.com

Printed in India at Vinayak Offset

This book is dedicated to...

My dear parents and children, it is through the words written in this book that I have realized how beautiful the journey of being a mother and an educator has been. It has shown me in the truest sense to accept and respect children as individual entities!

My mother who has always been my source of inspiration.

To my father who has encouraged my writing skills and given me a platform to express myself.

To my eldest brother who has been a role model to me.

To my Doctor brother who has taken me closer to my GOD.

To my husband and son who have made me more loving and patient as a person.

My special thanks to each one in my family at home and work for being a pillar of strength for me...

To my teacher Megha Bajaj who is further enhancing my expressions in writing.

And above all,

My heart felt DEEP Gratitude to my Revered Guru Mahatria, who has made me believe in myself and trust in GOD alone!

Introduction

When asked for an introduction to myself, I get into a fix! It leaves me with a question as to what should I say about myself?

So here is a humble attempt to do justice to my four decades of life on earth. Born as the youngest in the family with four elder brothers and me being the only sister, I was loved way beyond my imagination. I have heard stories that my mother was unable to believe that she was finally gifted with a daughter. Though this gave me an edge over my brothers, I did not take my parents love for granted and at every moment there was an earnest desire in me to make everyone proud of me.

Having grown in a conservative Marwari family a girl was expected to get married at a fairly young age (as soon as she turned eighteen). Being the odd one out, and a person who wanted to study and do something worthwhile in life, I continued to complete my graduation in Accountancy Honours from Kolkata. Fighting against many obstacles, I emerged to be the first girl who had graduated in the entire Kanoria family, with a desire to continue my studies further.

Marriage gave me an opportunity to study further and identify my passion of working with children. I completed my International Montessori Training from an Institute in

Kolkata which had direct affiliation with the London Montessori Centre. It was a one-year extensive degree course with serious studies, many projects and essays to be written. I enjoyed every moment of it and excelled in all the subjects.

The training had transformed me as a person. I understood that my passion to work with children can not only be out of love for children, but it has to be coupled with a realization. This was to "respect these tiny little ones as independent individuals with infinite potential." If we get this right, everything else becomes right. The training course was for a year and towards my final semester I was blessed to conceive.

The most exciting part was that the nine months of pregnancy seemed effortless to me and the most cherished period in my life. All the learnings were deep and meaningful. My son was learning what I was learning as a Montessorian. From excellence to orderliness; from patience to silence – some beautiful qualities were getting integrated naturally in our lives. This gave me an edge to start a Montessori House for children in 2002 when I moved to Chennai from Kolkata.

After having merged the Montessori House with a full-fledged school named Vatsalaya, I moved on to the application of all the knowledge I had accumulated. It started with helping others in the arena of Montessori and assessing papers as an examiner for The Institute where I had studied. During my training I had identified my skill in writing. We had to submit many papers on different subjects as thesis and I realized I enjoyed my tryst with words. With the encouragement of my father, I started an e-magazine for children with an audio/video interactive format. Children between 2 to 6 years have a very absorbent mind and are very sensitive to every stimulus in the environment. Keeping that as the focus of deliverance we moved ahead.

The e-magazine **iSpark Aspire to Inspire** was blessed by Dr. APJ Abdul Kalam on 14th January 2015 in RashtrapatiBhavan, Kolkata with his autograph and blessings for generating questioning in young minds to satiate their inner needs of curiosity. The mission of the magazine is to encourage children to Aspire to Inspire and keep moving ahead in life. In 2016, iSpark Holistic Happiness Studio was started in Chennai under the guidance of my father Dr. H.P. Kanoria and blessed by a Revered Soul.

My thirst for learning along with the children keeps growing at every moment and gets quenched as I translate all my learnings through words. The words are articulated through articles written in some life transforming magazines, business magazines as well as this child centric magazine called **iSpark Aspire to Inspire.**

As a seeker I have dwelled more in Silence which gives me immense patience with children and parents, to help them identify the spark in their child. As a Kathak dancer teaching young children has been my passion and as a yoga therapist I am able to live life with conscious awareness attaching myself only to GOD. My aim in life is to keep learning and growing, giving my BEST in every aspect and continue sharing my learnings through the gift of words.

Author's note

Ever since I had completed my International Montessori course from the London Montessori centre, I have been motivated to write articles for Business Economics and editorials in the e-magazine of I-Spark (I Spark is a Holistic Happiness Studio that I have founded in Chennai).

Inspired by the lives of great personalities like Swami Vivekananda and my beloved guru, Mahatria Ra, I have endeavored to write for the benefit of parents and children who are the ultimate beneficiaries of both my key ventures.

Thanks to my Montessori background along with the discipline I inculcated through my Kathak dance practices, I have dedicated my life around children and parents with a keen view to ensure that the upcoming generation is fully equipped with a sound body, mind and soul – which is the very essence of what we deliver at iSpark.

In the following pages, I have written extensively on all these lessons of life that I have embarked upon through my personal journey as an educator, a mother and as a seeker. I believe each one of us deserves a stress-free and fruitful existence and I pray that my words are gentle reminders to all towards the same.

Being gifted with a new day to live our life itself is nothing short of a miracle … and if we are to make it more meaningful, we must Aspire to Inspire ourselves and others around us.

My deepest gratitude to my parents for the spiritual upbringing that they bestowed upon me, to my brothers who are living inspirations, to my husband for his relentless support towards my dreams and to my son who has given birth to the mother in me. Above all, my humble obeisance to my Guru and God.

Hope you enjoy this compilation!

Manisha Lohia

Manisha Kanoria Lohia

Contents

1

Developing the Wings to Fly

"The greatness of the human personality begins
from the hour of birth."

– Maria Montessori.

Each child is endowed with unknown powers which can guide it towards a radiant future. Education can no longer be the giving of knowledge only; it must take on a different path. It is not just about what a teacher gives, but also about what a little one learns through his or her own individual experiences of life. Fact remains: If we want a new world then education must be as close to life in its lessons as possible.

"iSpark", as the name denotes is for each child to find their spark and realize its own potential and develop its personality. The activity and the information provided through the magazine caters to each child from a different angle. After all, the lens through which an eight-year-old child will perceive the magazine will differ from a fourteen-year-old teenager. The same information will be understood through unique viewpoints by each child. At the same time horizontal learning will take place around all age groups.

As such any reform of education must be based truly upon the development of the human personality as a whole. The child himself has to become the center of education and be empowered with "Wings to FLY".

The development starts from birth and in reality, even before birth. The greatest development takes place during the initial years of life and special care has to be taken during this period.

Rich information with good quality of pedagogy is instrumental in quenching the thirst of these young souls. Instead of ignoring the early years, it is our duty to cultivate them with utmost care enabling the child to reveal himself as the greatest marvel of nature.

We, as teachers and parents, can only help the great work being done, as servants would wait upon the masters. If we do so, we shall witness the unfolding of the human soul to the rising of a New Man who is not a victim of events, but will rather have the clarity of vision to direct and shape the future of human society.

My dear young friends, I urge you all to dream big, dream noble and draw all the right vibrations and keep aspiring to inspire.

Like the famous saying of author, Paulo Coelho:

"When you want something, the entire universe conspires in helping you to achieve it."

The world needs you.

2

A Tribute

"Education is the most powerful weapon which you can use to change the world."

– Dr A P J Kalam

Our beloved Former President Professor Dr. A P J Abdul Kalam kept urging young children to dream big and to work hard to fulfill their aspirations. He always linked individual aspirations with the greatness of the nation. His utter simplicity, coupled with shunning of pomp and show, touched the hearts of millions of people in a society, so used to misusage of power.

He was truly a source of inspiration to me. The couple of times that I was blessed to have met him, I started aspiring towards contributing towards development of young minds. This is when the thought of starting a children's magazine using technology sprouted in my mind. The e-magazine, iSpark is an inspiration gathered from the Montessori philosophy by emphasizing oneness of everything in the universe. It also believes in tapping the individual potential of the child. **"iSpark: Aspire to Inspire"**, has been created with this vision to empower children to appreciate their roots by going within, as well as to have the courage to go beyond imagination and find their wings in the world outside. We also hope to pique their curiosity and capitalize on their desire to become something of significance in the future.

The e-magazine aims to stimulate the intellectual abilities of children by educating them about their origin, and to reflect upon various topics to them from different perspectives. With the wide usage of technical gadgets amongst children, our magazine is an attempt to kindle the spark within them to maximize learning opportunities through technology. The magazine has been designed with an audio-video format where the children can enhance their learning skills through both visual and auditory senses. In this time and age, children after their birth immediately adapt to technology and respond to it most appropriately.

Recently, we lost a great soul but he will live with us and his teaching within us. Former President Professor A P J Abdul Kalam's vision was to ignite the minds of children across the globe. Come, let us carry forward his torch in our own child's life, by helping them to flap their wings and fly.

"I will fly and fly
I am born with potential.
I am born with goodness and trust.
I am born with ideas and dreams.
I am born with greatness.
I am born with confidence.
I am born with wings.
So, I am not meant for crawling,
I have wings, I will fly
I will fly and fly."

3

Nurturing Blossoms in the Family Garden

"This is the only chance you have got to be you,
Do not accept anyone's definition of life,
Define it yourself..."

– Mahatria Ra

Children are like the buds of a flower, blooming and blossoming at every step. As parents we are only the means through which God sends them into the universe. We are nothing but a mere tiny speck of dust in this Galaxy, our Milky Way. There are many more such specks and in order to stand out and be looked upon, we have to do something remarkable!

We, as parents, contribute in the making of our child. Aligning them to the right values, behaviors and attitudes is a major responsibility and should be done happily. We are like gardeners in a child's life. A gardener takes care of the plants, waters them, and nourishes them; consistently pulls out the weeds, so each sapling can grow into a magnificent tree and bear fruits.

It is my humble belief that God has carefully chosen parents to act as gardeners, by aiding the overall development of the child and nourishing them with good thoughts and vibrations. Here development implies the physical, mental, intellectual and spiritual development.

The more happily, and efficiently, that we "garden" our young ones, the more beautiful will be the future of the world.

Let's get this right, dear parents and educators!

BE AN EXAMPLE

"Clothes lying here and there,
Such a mess, do you care!
Pick up, arrange will you so dear?"
As I lay down cozily on my chair.

Books spread on the table,
Television running through the cable
Everything seems to be unstable,
And I suddenly started to stumble.

"What sort of scene is this?
Come, let us arrange them with bliss"
I spoke to my young lad with a kiss
And asked him to quickly dismiss.

Are we an example or a threat?
To prove to our young ones to sweat,
To feel worthy of every stead!
And make them deserve THE Respect.

4

Inspired by his Wings of Fire

"Educating the mind without educating the heart is no education at all."

– Aristotle

Parents are the first teachers in the lives of children. The first sound that a child hears, while in the womb, is that of its mother. The mother, by the law of nature, is the first teacher for the child and introduces it to its father. GRATITUDE must be an integral part of the child's life for the mother and father. Have you noticed? All great people who have achieved humongous feats have always expressed their immense gratitude towards their parents.

5th of September is celebrated as Teacher's Day in India to mark the integral role that a mentor plays in the child's life. Starting from this Teacher's Day, and henceforth, may we all first express gratitude towards our parents who are our first ever teachers. 'Matha' (mother) comes first, then 'Pitha' (father), followed by 'Guru' (teacher) and finally 'Deivam' (God). The mother shows the father to the child, parents guide the child to the teacher (Guru), and the Guru reveals God to it.

On Teacher's Day, children learn to express gratitude to these forces who have been instrumental in igniting the spark of life, love and learning within them.

On this special day, I cannot help but mention Prof. Dr. A P J Abdul Kalam who was the former President of India and a legendary teacher. I pay my humble obeisance to him for encouraging the youth to ASPIRE and follow their dreams. I remember reading in his book, 'Wings of Fire', which said that when one aspires for something with a true heart and sows a seed for it in the environment, in the darkness of the night, those particles create vibrations for it to be achieved.

Prof. Dr. A P J Abdul Kalam will live in the hearts of many who valued him as their mentor, teacher and guide. India mourns the loss of such an exceptional gem who not just led by words, but by example. He was a person with unquenchable curiosity and utmost humility.

It is very rare to find a person who was a source of unimaginable knowledge and who inspired an entire generation of youngsters. He made them believe in themselves and aroused confidence in them to aspire for the stars. He himself was an exceptionally bright and hardworking student who toiled under the guidance of illustrious teachers like Vikram Sarabhai (known as the greatest scientist of India and father of Indian Space Program). Popularly known as The missile man of India, the eleventh president of India, Dr. A P J Abdul Kalam (receiver of the prestigious Bharat Ratna) will always live in our hearts and make us believe that we are indeed born with "Wings of Fire!"

Children are the future of the nation as quoted by Professor Kalam. By educating them and imparting moral values in them, a new world can be created. As adults, each one of us has to set an example for children to emulate. The role of a teacher is indispensable for the child to develop a love for the subject. When this happens, the child is empowered to love and respect the teacher as well. With a loving and yet stern and disciplined approach the teacher can empower the child to lead a well-balanced life.

It is very important for teachers to follow what they say else they will be a failure in creating an impact. They should have this absolute belief in each child's potential, that one day they will make it very big in life. A beautiful master-disciple relationship was one that was shared between Sri Ramakrishna Paramahansa and Swami Vivekananda. The faith which Sri Ramakrishna Paramahansa had in Narendra, made him a Swami Vivekananda; the surrender which Swami Vivekananda had for his master was unparalleled and can be spoken for generations to come.

The soil of India has given us legendary people to look up to and I pray for each child to develop a deep love for their teachers. This will for sure help them to draw miraculous possibilities into their lives. With the blessings of their teachers they will be able to STAND OUT IN THE CROWD.

I feel proud to have lived in the time of a great teacher like Professor Dr. A P J Abdul Kalam. May his blessings for the magazine continue to ignite young minds!

5

Good Teaching Shapes the Character

"The brightest star is yourself. Get your position right, everything will fall into place."

– Unknown

My dear young friends, this is a month when India will be celebrating an array of festivals. To mark the beginning of the month, it is our beloved Bapu's birthday. The contribution made by Mahatma Gandhi to make India free from British rule is monumental. Let us dwell back into the past and reflect into his life. What inspired an ordinary barrister to emerge as the Father of the Nation?

Mohandas Karamchand Gandhi, more commonly known as "Mahatma" meaning "Great Soul," was not a great scholar, nor was he a great warrior. He was neither born with exceptional faculties; nor was he a good orator. He was yet another ordinary human being. However, what made him believe that he was not meant for ordinary things in life was his own BELIEF IN HIMSELF. We are what we make of ourselves. Each one of us is endowed with different intellectual and mental faculties. How we use it, defines our life.

Gandhiji said "My life is my message." I would like to share a few instances from his life which are bound to inspire our young readers. It's interesting to know that Gandhi studied law at the University College of London strictly adhering to the Hindu principles of vegetarianism and alcohol and sexual abstinence. He chose not to let the environment or peer pressure affect him – and stood his ground under all circumstances.

He was greatly inspired to pursue the philosophical study of religions including Hinduism, Christianity, Buddhism and others. He moved to South Africa for a few years to practice as a Barrister and railed against the injustice of racial segregation. On one such occasion while travelling to South Africa, he was thrown out from a first class train carriage despite possessing a valid ticket. He felt absolutely humiliated. This was a turning point in his life, "A Breakthrough Moment" which served as a catalyst for his later activism. Instead of sulking or complaining as to why something like this had happened to him, he chose to let the incident inspire the rest of his life.

He encouraged the villagers in Bihar who were oppressed by the British Masters to improve their circumstances by leading peaceful strikes and protests. With this he started the non-violence movement which brought fame to him nationally and he was widely referred as "Mahatma", the Great Soul. Finally, India got freedom from the British rule with Gandhi's Quit India Movement through this novel approach of non-violence.

How was all of this possible? Only because Gandhiji believed in himself and was confident that evil can be vanquished with peace. He had to struggle and prove his point till the last breath but he never gave up. His life is a message to all of us that if we dare to take up something which we believe in, let us have the power to follow it. If we do, monumental results are possible!

Like Swami Vivekananda said, *"Take up one idea, make that one idea your life, think of it, dream of it. Live on that idea. Let the brain, muscles, nerves, every part of your body be full of that idea and just leave every other idea alone. This is the way to success."*

All the great souls who have walked on the rich soil of our country India have set an example in their own way for each one of us to follow, a path which uniquely befits us respecting each other's values.

My Dear young ones, let us "Awake and Arise" and dare to do something outstanding in this life so that in the coming years our birthdays too are also remembered by all. When we are no longer embodied in this physical form we will be remembered for our contributions towards our motherland and to humanity as a whole.

Are you ready? I sure am...

6

Tentative Steps to Steady Strides

My Dear young friends, I wish all of you a very Happy Children's Day as well as a fun filled Deepavali. Mark this Children's Day to be a turning point in your life. May you be able to draw in humongous possibilities from all directions. I wish to reiterate to you something which my Beloved Guru Mahatria says, "*If you do your best, He will take care of the rest. If you do not do your best, He will take rest.*"

I am implementing this is in my life and I can see a spectacular change in the way He is taking care of everything. I wish that all the young ones reading this should put it in practice from this very moment.

Let us start with the way you "study". Be regular with your studies, give in your best and believe me, He will take care of the rest. You will emerge as a "Numero Uno". Whatever you take up, feel involved, feel engrossed, do it with enthusiasm and you will feel a miraculous change. What do you mean by "enthusiasm"? It is derived from the Greek word "enthos" which means "to be in touch with God."

Children's Day has a very special place in my heart. On this day we celebrate the birthday of Pandit Jawaharlal Nehru who was the first Prime Minister of Independent India. He was extremely fond of both children and roses. He compared the two often by saying that children are like the buds in a garden ... they should be carefully and lovingly nurtured. They are the future of the nation and the citizens of tomorrow. He was adored by the children of India who gave him the endearing name of "Chacha Nehru."

A small note to all parents and adults here. Children are the real strength of the country and the very foundation of society. What we do as parents will make them blossom. If we give attention to negative seeds, we will be developing those qualities in them. What we focus on, will grow! Instead, let us focus on the positive seeds and develop their strengths. If we accept a child as it is and direct our attention to what it can do, it will help it to grow much more, than if we focus on what it cannot do.

Another thing we need to bear in mind as parents is the need to respect every child and love them the way they are. Each child is different, unique and has his own personality. Comparing the child with others retards his growth. Each child is wired to grow, learn and flourish in a unique way and we need to internalize this.

Let us take the example of a baby who is learning to walk. He takes a tentative step forward, looks at his parents with a proud smile, takes another step and then, maybe even falls down. He laughs, clambers up again to take a few steps and then again falls down. This goes on for some time till he is tired/sleepy and, after a good rest, starts all over again. There is no sense of embarrassment, shame or self-doubt. So, where does it all start going wrong?

Using the same example of the baby here, if we tell the

baby to try harder, make sure he bends forward, or that if he straightens his knees a little or looks forward, he might move better or if we started comparing his steps to our friend's daughter who, at the same age, is running what would happen? I am sure he might give up very soon and not want to try much. We might feel that his lack of effort is because he does not want to try, wants to take the easy way out, is simply lazy, or wants to waste his life doing nothing. But that is exactly what we are doing with our grown up children. Whenever they stop trying or moving forward we want to immediately label them without finding out the cause behind it.

Parenting cannot be generalized and I do believe each parent is different like each child is wired and inspired differently. I feel parenting is not JUST BRINGING UP CHILDREN. It is about growing up and transforming ourselves to be better human beings. What could be more beautiful than learning from our own children? In my own experience as a mother first, and as a Montessori teacher, along with being a Kathak trainer for young girls, I feel I have learnt maximum from the close proximity that I have shared with each child.

As a mother, every moment with my son has been a delightful experience. I have gone through so many wonderful and learning experiences as a parent that I believe motherhood is one of the best things that I was blessed with!

In the Montessori environment, I have experienced children between two to six years move beautifully without disturbing each other, showing deep interest in learning, working independently, caring for each other, fighting and then again loving each other spontaneously.

As a Kathak teacher, I observed young girls aged from eight to thirteen years immediately picking up the subtle nuances of dancing. However, once the learning took place, it would go deep into their subconscious mind and at any moment if I forgot something, they would be there to gently remind me.

As my Beloved Guru Mahatria says: there are seven layers of the subconscious mind and only one layer of the conscious mind. We must train ourselves such that our subconscious mind becomes more powerful than the conscious mind. As children it is very easy to train the subconscious mind and make any learning become a "learning for life." I sometimes feel deep wonderment about the beautiful innate nature of children. Why cannot we become like them? So innocent, so happy, so loving, so mischievous, so connected to the Divine and hence so pure! The problems in the world shall cease to exist, once we accept that within each one of us truly there is a child.

On this Children's Day I wish to reiterate to all the parents and adults to make a paradigm shift to not delve in the realm of teaching at all times and instead start the process of learning from our children. To all my young readers here, I wish to reiterate to you to START PUTTING IN YOUR BEST and GOD WILL TAKE CARE OF THE REST.

Happy Children's Day. To all the children. And to every adult who carries a child-like enthusiasm to learn!

7

Let's Grow?

To all my young friends, wishing you a life full of unexplored possibilities and more! As we are approaching the end of the year, it is time to review and make certain changes for improvement.

As Revered Mahatria says,

> *"That which does not change, does not grow.*
> *That which does not grow, dies.*
> *Grow we must. So, change we must.*
> *Growth and change are inseparable."*

We have to keep changing and setting new benchmarks for ourselves and consistently keep moving to the next step. To keep growing we must set goals larger than ourselves and inspire our children to keep aspiring. Children are the future of the nation. They have a lot within themselves which when tapped in the right direction, can help them to utilize their individual potential to the fullest. We, as parents and teachers, are instrumental in shaping the lives of our children.

With the beginning of the New Year, let us change and grow to be perfect role models for them. Children learn much more from what they see, than what they hear. The way we behave and conduct ourselves, registers in their subconscious minds and they carry it forward. This can be compared to the bee which carries nectar from one flower to the other. When they interact with the world with positive qualities, it fills their lives with the desired results which is like "honey" from the beehive.

As parents we must understand that each child is different. They need not fit into the so-called group we want them to be classified in. It is said that we need to look at the glass as half full and not half empty. I would like to go a step further and say that don't focus on the glass – which is half full or empty – just celebrate the sparkling water. Let us change the spectacles through which we see our children, and help them to develop a beautiful insight into themselves. We are only the means through which they come into the universe. They have a purpose in life which will be defined by them in their own special way. We have to believe in them.

Let us ignite the spark in them to keep growing.

Let us help them to keep flowing.

AHA! CHILDREN

They say after we are no more
Embodied in flesh and blood
We become like a star
Lighting up the sky which adds
Infinite beauty to the darkness
That surrounds the universe!

I compare this analogy with
Children, AHA! *Children.*
Do they not add infinite beauty?

In our lives, lighting up everything
Around and within us
Igniting the child in us to spark...

Their smile, their touch,
Their words, does it not feel
God Himself has descended
To earth, cast a magical wand
On each one of us
To transform in HIS spell!

I say *Children* by far are the most
Sensitive of all beings,
Spreading their innocence and charm
In all lives they touch.
Leaving a trace of their purity
For us to become divine too!

Sitting near my window sill,
As I admirethe dark sky
With its immaculate beauty
With an array of shining stars
An ever-longing desire arises
To become one like them!

To be ever remembered
As MYSELF...as learnt from
Children, Aha Children!

8

You Reap What You Sow

Wishing a very Happy New Year to all my young readers friends! May this New Year be a benchmark to all the years that have passed by and enrich your life with beautiful experiences. An inspiring thought quoted by Swami Vivekananda crosses my mind as we step into another purposeful year:

"Take up one idea, make that one idea your life, think of it, dream of it, live on that idea. Let the brain, muscles, nerves, every part of your body, be full of that idea, just leave every other idea alone this is the way to success."

Anything and everything is possible if we work with unquestionable determination and sincere efforts. All the great leaders from our country and from other parts of the world have stood on the ladder of success by passionately living up to that "one idea."

My dear children, while you are still young start focusing on any one aspect which kindles a spark within you. Focus on something that makes you happy. That, which you can keep doing tirelessly, is your "Purpose". Aspire to do something outstanding in life for which you will always be remembered. Each one of us has a special characteristic trait which defines us and distinguishes us from others. Each animal has a particular tendency, each plant is different from another and every flower has a specific aromatic smell. We, as Human Beings have been created by God to create something unique, something which will add meaning to life itself.

Let us attempt to create a better world. This is possible only when you start young. We offer fresh flowers to God, not stale ones. So also, children are like fresh flowers offered at the altar of God.

Dear children, you have to start dreaming; dream big, dream high, dream to reach the stars one day. Very soon you shall see your dreams shaping into reality. My Beloved Guru says that whatever thought we implant into the universe, it becomes vibrations. These vibrations have the power to attract or repel. If we have pure thoughts, the entire universe will conspire for its fulfillment. While unwanted thoughts will get repelled by themselves.

It is very important to focus on the company we seek for our children. Parents play a very important role in this. We must encourage them to be with high energy people, to read autobiographies of eminent personalities and listen to the sermons of evolved souls. As the famous saying goes "What you sow, you reap." If you plant an orange tree, you will get oranges; if you plant an apple tree, you will get apples. If we as parents instill hard work, determination, faith and effort in our children from a very young age, they will grow up with these qualities.

It is my firm belief that a parent should never think wrong for the child. Especially what the mother wishes for her child becomes a command to the universe. Let us focus on the strengths of our children and always be a role model worth emulating for them. Our children will slowly be drawn towards success in whatever they aspire for.

Whatever you do, do it with utmost intensity and put every part of your mind to it like the above quote of Swami Vivekananda says. This will have no choice but to yield THE BEST results which will lead to SUCCESS. I would like to reiterate to all the children to start internalizing this quote every single day in this year.

Charaiveti Charaiveti, keep going, keep going...

9

Face the Future Fearlessly

The year 2016 has set in beautifully. Let us march into the second month with grit, determination and optimism to target realistic goals and achieve them successfully. I would like to quote a few words from a Universal Prayer as written by my father, Dr. H.P. Kanoria –

"O God! Thou art our Father, Mother, Friend! We, thy children, love thee and our parents. Thou art in our hearts and minds. Make us fearless."

When the intention is pure and the goal is upliftment of ourselves and others, then surely, without any doubt, one will receive guidance from positive and benevolent forces all around us. Many of our prophets and great masters believed in the above saying.

My dear children, it is very important for us to love God and always feel Him within us. This will give us the courage to face anything in life and be fearless.

Like Revered Mahatria says, "FACE ANYTHING IN TRUSTING HIM – FAITH."

No matter what you may go through – one thing you have to remember is to remain true to your "Self". Have you ever pondered upon the fact, "Who you are?" or "What this Self is?" I often wondered upon this as a child.

I think the answer actually changes life as we see it, forever. For we are not the clothes we wear or the thoughts we hold – we are the reflection of God! Him and we are made in the same image. We have to exhibit God-like qualities if we are made in His image.

When we read about the lives of people who have made a difference to mankind, our mind expands. Childhood is the best age to develop a strong foundation which in turn forms the base for our lives. Reading inspiring stories and books shapes the mind in a positive way. It provides lessons about life that lies outside our own personal experiences.

You cannot change the environment in which you were born and raised. There is a limit to the number of people you can meet in the course of your life. However, through books and novels written by great writers, you can learn about the lives of people who lived in totally different environments, or times. Further, by identifying yourself with real life heroes you will learn more deeply about their lives. All the great people have become great because their intentions were pure and their goal was higher and much larger than themselves.

So my mantra for all the young ones is "Read, Read and Read." My aspirations are that one day you will also become great and someone (including me) will read about your life and get inspired and feel proud.

Waiting for that day, and how!

10

Be a Role Model for Children

My dear young friends, as we enter into the month of March – the month of exams I cannot help but say to each one of you: let's surpass our own expectations and stand apart!

As we move on to the next grade/next stage let us always be prepared to welcome new challenges and approach them confidently. We are the product of our own thoughts and desires, and in that sense each one of us is our own architect. We have such a great power at our disposal, yet the irony is that we fail to use it. We are the cause of everything that happens to us. Stephen Covey says:

"The best way to predict your future is to create it."

Dear parents, I firmly believe in the power of Silence and meditation. Children should be introduced to this at a very young age as this will enable them to flow through challenging periods, or times of transition, with ease and grace. The Silence which the child experiences while in the womb of the mother should be retained when he comes into enters the real world.

Have you ever thought as to why the child cries after birth? The answer is very simple! So far he was in darkness, in Silence, cocooned in the mother's womb. Suddenly, as he comes into the world he feels insecure and cries out aloud to go back into the place of quietude. We come from Silence and dissolve back into it. Meditativeness is our inborn nature. We lose it as soon as we come into the outer world. We must empower our children to reconnect with their original state through powerful tools like yoga, chanting, meditation, introspection and self-awareness.

What we are born with is our greatest asset, but we rarely realize it. We spend so much of our time only comparing ourselves with others and getting into the rat race of trying to be like someone else. Why do we try to be like others? God has given us such a wonderful person called "myself" which resides in each one of us. If we love and accept ourselves as we are, then life becomes so easy and uncomplicated. We can work on ourselves to keep improving and progressing rather than wasting time on meaningless comparisons!

Here again I want to emphasize on a very important aspect. What we teach our children from a young age gets embedded in them. We can create them or destroy them. Parents and teachers play a very important role in the lives of children. They have to identify the "spark" within each child and help them to achieve their goals and ambitions. The whole drama of comparing unfortunately starts from home, when we create comparisons between two or more children.

Does this sound familiar? "He is so good at singing, why are you not?" I wish the child would reply, "Yes Maa, I understand that my brother is good in music, but I am good in dance." God has given us five fingers, all in varied size, but when we close it, it becomes a fist and that is more powerful than any one finger. Likewise, each child is born with a special capability. If we can become instrumental in helping the child understand his own strength, then there will be no scope for comparison. This world which is already beautiful, will become a better place to live in and we shall be able to create hundreds and thousands of "young achievers."

Our children deserve only the best of us. Let's give it to them?

11

Life is a Dream

Dream Dream Dream
Dreams transform into thoughts
And thoughts result in action!

Dr. A.P.J Abdul Kalam has beautifully said, *"Children, if there are no dreams, there are no revolutionary thoughts; if there are no thoughts, no actions will emanate. Hence, parents and teachers should allow their children to dream. Success always follows dreams attempted, though there may be some setbacks and delays."*

With the onset of the summer heat all over the country, let our children spend more time indoors and rediscover themselves through their dreams. Dr. Kalam was a role model to all the young minds in the way he lived his life with utmost simplicity and humility. He felt that the only way he could transcend himself and discover his own inner, higher self was through his interactions with joyous children.

It is hard for us to find one true "Vidura" among our leaders. Vidura was a character in the famous epic of Mahabharata who displayed grit against the wrongdoings of authority and had the courage to differ when everyone else chose to surrender before the tyranny of injustice. It is difficult to find such a true and enlightened person in the universe.

How many such leaders can we vouch for in our country, India and more so in the world now? Should we not aim and dedicate our lives in creating such heroes?

This is a question I would like to ask all the parents and teachers here. Can we not live by such values and principles ourselves so that our children, who come through us, will be able to imbibe these values almost instinctively? The environment in which they grow has to be extremely conducive to this. Just as heredity is a key factor in determining the behavioral patterns of children, as important is the role played by the environment. As Revered Mahatria says, *"Children learn more from what they see, than from what they hear."* The mother, father and the school teachers play a very important role in the lives of children. They shoulder a very big, yet the most wonderful, responsibility to impart the best guidance unto them.

What more can we, as parents want, than to create and nurture these young minds which are filled with an innate quest for life which only time can unfold? It is extremely important for every parent to help their children to identify their dreams, as early in life as possible and help them to work towards them.

In my growing years, I used to see my mother worshipping and offering her prayers to God and ensuring all her five children did the same before they left for school. My father who was always very hard-working, ensured that we ate healthy food and offered the same to any child who came to our house. I remember him telling my mother very often, "Even if there is less food and if a neighboring child comes to our home, you must let our children share with them." He did go through a financial crisis but never stopped giving to the needy around him through whatever little resources he had.

My point here is to make all the parents aware of this Truth, *"What they do or do not do, children will unconsciously imbibe everything from them."* If we have decided to become parents, we have to execute the "Dharma" of a parent else we do not have any right to become a parent. We do not have any right to bring into existence another life and not be instrumental in creating that life.

The role which the school teachers play is equally important, as they help in creating leaders out of children. The teacher is the child's window to learning and knowledge. If parents and teachers show the required dedication in shaping these young lives, we will soon be living in a new India, and a new world at large.

With this, I would like to conclude leaving behind a message to my dear children and young readers:

Dream, Dream and Dream...

Whatever you do must come from your heart,

Express your spirit and keep radiating,

Love and Joy in abundance!

12

Dreams Can be Achieved

I take great pride in sharing with all of you, dear friends, that "iSpark" completes one year this month. The e-magazine has been blessed by none other than our former president Professor A P J Abdul Kalam on 14th January, 2014, a very auspicious day in the Indian calendar. Sacred it is, as people celebrate this day as the day of harvest "Pongal" in southern India and as "Makar Sakranti" in the northern part of India.

For me it is precious as my dream of being instrumental in making a difference in the lives of children came true. It was my desire to conceptualize something for children as my first initiative and it being blessed by Dr. Kalam (who for me is the symbol of love, simplicity and humility) was indeed a moment to cherish!

From Kalam Sir I learnt humility in being rooted to the ground as we keep soaring heights. Born in the fishing hamlets of Rameshwaram, he has inspired the lives of many, including mine. The first meeting with him in the President House in New Delhi had a great impact on me. Whenever I was in Delhi, I would request my father to arrange a meeting with him. Every interaction with him ignited yet another 'spark' within me to contribute to the lives of children in a holistic way.

Whatever one dreams and aspires to achieve, gets fulfilled if there is an earnest desire associated with it which has a larger objective and not just a personal one. The entire universe conspires for it and makes the dreams shape into reality. This is absolutely true for me, and my dream for "iSpark". I simply dreamt and dreamt earnestly as to how children could use technology to do something more creative than just play games, watch videos and the like. I thought to myself that if children want to use electronic gadgets then let me provide them with a platform which will be a ready source of education as well as entertainment for them.

My dear young readers, I would again request you as in the note for the month of April, "Delve into the realm of dreaming, dreaming and dreaming. Make all the necessary efforts in that direction and then leave the result on that Infinite force which pervades the entire universe. Be sure with faith that your efforts will never go in 'vain'."

Come the month of May, and the parents have innumerable thoughts of how the children should use the warmest period of the year productively. Looking out for summer camp, taking a short break, investing more time as a family and above all staying well-hydrated and comfortably clothed are predominant thoughts in any parent's mind, I am sure! I feel summer holidays are the best time of the year where children can discover their innate hidden talents by trying to tap their creative abilities. As Revered Mahatria says:

"Use yourself fully, you will be "USEFUL". Use yourself less, you will be "USELESS"!

The world-renowned Nineteenth-Century-African-American social reformer Frederick Douglas wrote, *"It is easier to build strong children than to repair broken men."* The learning for life starts when the children are just born and goes on till they complete six years of age. Most of the learning in the life of an individual takes place between the ages of 2 to 6 years. Unconsciously children pick up every stimulus from the time they are born. In fact, learning takes place right from the time they are in the womb of the mother. Exposing them to right sounds and right words is extremely important and this holds true for them every summer too. Please do not allow them to while their precious time away!

Summer is the time to re-create, I hope you use this one well!

13

New Beginnings

June is the month to start afresh with a new academic year, to strive to put our best foot forward. My dear children, start with fresh vigor and vitality, outperform and surpass your own expectations.

Keep developing, keep aspiring for what next, what more, keep moving, keep going. As my Revered Guru Mahatria keeps saying, *"Go On. Do not halt. Do not stagnate. Rest not. Keep going..."*

My dear parents, let us learn to nurture our children more intelligently and lovingly from this academic year. As the Lebanese poet Kahlil Gibran wrote:

Your children are not your children.

They are the sons and daughters of Life's longing for itself.

They come through you but not from you,

And though they are with you yet they belong not to you.

Let's treat each new academic year as a chance to become more patient, more loving, less doubting and critical of our little ones. When they watch us renewing ourselves, they will want to do it too!

It's the first day, to the rest of my life... can we see each day in June with this fresh perspective?

14

Happiness is Living in the Moment

"Keep loving nature and care for its blessings.
Then you can see divinity all over"

– A. P. J Abdul Kalam

My dear children and young friends, may you always keep aspiring for most and more in your lives. Never be content with what you have done, always have an aspiration to go a step further in your lives from where you are. The question is not from "where to where" but from "here where" as my beloved guru Mahatria says.

As children we are all very loving and filled with inexhaustible energy. However, when we grow up, emotions of anger, jealousy, lust starts playing a dominant role in our lives. If you have seen children playing, you will see at one moment they are fighting with each other, but the very next moment they are once again friends, giggling with mirth.

I must say that all of us must take some time out to do one of these: Take a walk down a park or just go sit near the beach. It is the most beautiful of all experiences to simply see the children playing with each other. With absolute abandon, they go about shrieking in glee, running around, at times falling on the ground deliberately and laughing at their own folly;

sometimes merrily chasing a butterfly, the next moment picking up some sand and throwing at each other. Ah! What a Divine sight indeed! I am sure even the Heavenly Gods would be in awe to behold such a sight.

Now the question is why as we grow up, do we get engulfed with negative emotions and miss out on the small and beautiful aspects of life? Can we not have the nature of a child, always happy, loving, full of joy and excitement? We can attempt to do a few simple things which can make us feel even more alive. For instance, I feel investing time in nature reconnects us to ourselves. Have you ever felt the joy of just gazing out of the window and looking at the skies?

There seems to exist an immense expansiveness in nature which never ends. This gives us a sense of 'joy'. All the natural forces are so much in tune with each other. The sun rises and sets at a particular time in the day, the birds keep chirping, the bud blooms into a flower spontaneously when the appropriate time comes, the bees keep giving us the divine nectar through the flowers and the stream keeps flowing (in a never ending journey of life).

Our children come into existence through us and we shoulder a beautiful responsibility in creating them and giving back to the world as creations with emulating. Let us do it happily and lovingly. Let us once again become like a child. By becoming a child, I mean to say become child-like in our behavior, in the way we look at life with deep positive feelings and associations.

Have you ever seen a child depressed? The answer is a loud resounding NO! Even if a child weeps – it is for that moment alone. Within a short time span they are back to their mischief and bliss! The reason for their unbounded enthusiasm is that they live their life in the present. They sip happily from every moment and nothing seems to matter to them beyond that. What one says, what one does or what one does not, plays no importance in their lives. We, as parents, fathom and hold on to so many things in our minds which unconsciously gets transferred to our children. Let us for once get in touch with the free, spontaneous child within each one of us and connect with the God residing within us. This will for sure make us live life 'happily and lovingly' in the present moment. These two words have played a very important role in my life. Revered Mahatria aptly shares:

"Where there is love and happiness, there is PEACE,
Where there is PEACE, there is SILENCE,
Where there is SILENCE, GOD descends."

Parenting is an inside out job. For that we have to calm our chattering mind and connect with the deep wisdom within. This can only happen when we as parents learn to observe Silence. This will give us the power to control our emotions. Children are very receptive and sensitive to the emotions of their parents. We, as parents, have to be very cautious with the words we use. Derogatory words lower our 'prana', 'chi' or energy. I feel it is impossible to be offensive and spiritually aware at the same time. Why not constantly choose the latter?

Children thrive when they feel appreciated, recognized and valued as human beings. Recognition is about nourishing the heart and soul of the child with words of acceptance, love and praise.

There is a reason we were chosen as care-givers. Let us do the best that we can!

15

Let Success Stem from Within

"EVERY CHILD IS AN ARTIST"

– Pablo Picasso

Walk the unexplored path,
Follow an untrodden path,
Fearlessly with indomitable courage;
And strive to be UNIQUE.

My heart swells in gratitude for Professor A. P. J Abdul Kalam. Although he departed from his earthly body on the twenty seventh of July, 2015, he continues to live in my heart. As I sit down to pen down a few of my thoughts on the Editor's note for 'iSpark', my eyes fill with tears remembering a few personal interactions with him. I feel I can endlessly keep sharing about the deep impact his words had made on me. He had written and blessed the magazine with his encouraging and motivating words 'My best wishes for generating questioning and questioning'.

Ever since I had conceptualized the idea of starting a magazine for children, it was my earnest desire to receive his blessings. His greatest passion was to inspire and uplift the youth and the children. I know with the blessings of a genuine soul like him, this magazine, so close to my heart, will take off to greater heights and touch and inspire millions of children all around the globe.

Isn't it miraculous that Dr Kalam breathed his last while doing what he was most passionate about? If we also channelize our passions in the right direction with determination, grit, hard work and above all a noble heart, we will soon be writing our own success story.

If we learn to study ourselves and introspect daily we would not have to go to any institution or read books on how to become SUCCESSFUL, we will become a SUCCESS by ourselves. Dr. Kalam came from a very humble background, where his father had a noble mind and was a good human being. His father had taught him an extremely valuable lesson while he was still very young: 'Never accept a gift from anyone which comes under the cover of a purpose through which one may lose one's integrity.'

My dear children, I would request all of you to limit your expectations from others and turn your hopes and aspirations towards yourself. Fight the hardest battle to retain your uniqueness and don't be lost in the crowds. We are a soul of God, garbed in His image to carry forward a mission for our own lives which is solely designed for us. How God conspires every move for us, we do not know, but when our intentions are pure and comes from a genuine heart, everything works in alignment to make our wishes come true.

'Preserve your Divine Light.' In the word 'Preserve', there is a hidden word: 'serve'. Serve means to do 'seva'... that is to serve ourselves and others. We can serve ourselves by striving to develop important human traits of righteousness, courage, vision, indomitable spirit, hard work, commitment, team spirit, magnanimity, truthfulness and honesty within us. Kalam sir was described to stand out as having the honesty of a child, the energy of adolescence and the maturity of an adult. As quoted by him,

"Everyone has inside of him or her, a piece of good news.
The good news is, that you don't know how great you can be!"

In our journey towards greatness, it is very important to pay careful attention to the relationships we build, to form connections with the noble and the pious. We feel happy when we offer fresh flowers as offering to God. Children are those fresh flowers. They have an absorbent mind and are like a 'blotting paper'. If we associate them with negative minded people those tendencies will rub on them. As the famous saying goes, *"As iron sharpens iron, so one person sharpens another."*

To conclude with what Revered Mahatria says:

"Target the stars,
In case you miss the target,
You will surely reach the clouds!"

16

Parents are the First Teachers

My dear young friends, the beginning of the month of September celebrates Teachers Day across India. September 5th marks the birthday of Dr. S. Radhakrishnan, the second President of India. Pandit Jawaharlal Nehru, who was one of his closest friends said about Dr. Radhakrishnan: *"He has served his country in many capacities. But above all, he is a great Teacher from whom all of us have learnt much and will continue to learn. It is India's privilege to have a great philosopher, a great educationist and a great humanist as its President. That in itself shows the kind of men we honour and respect."* Bharat Ratna, the highest award of the nation, was conferred on him in 1954 in recognition of his meritorious service to mankind.

A brief reflection on the life of Dr. Radhakrishnan is to create an awareness for our young readers, that indeed our country is blessed with many such wonderful teachers. We only have to acknowledge the presence of such beings who devote their lives to service and for the upliftment of mankind through the medium of education. I feel so proud to be a citizen of India where we learn to appreciate every small gesture displayed by others. As the African word "Ubuntu" so profoundly suggests: *"I am what I am because of who we all are."*

In fact, India has contributed immensely to the world in many fields which has been developed by the western countries and again handed back to us. One such contribution is the game of 'Snakes and Ladders' which we all must have played as children. Did we ever think how this game evolved? It was developed by a 13th century poet Gyandev as 'ParamaPadama or Mokshapat' to inculcate important values of life in a game format for children. It was further renamed by the Britishers as "Snakes and Ladders."

Here the Ladders represent the 'virtues' while the Snakes represent the 'vices'. Our evil tendencies or our animalistic nature is like a snake which when bites us, pulls us down in life indicating our 'vices'. God-like tendencies and our Divine qualities have an upward spiral and takes us much higher in life like a ladder which indicates our 'virtues'. We, as parents and teachers, shoulder a huge responsibility towards guiding the children towards the right path.

By celebrating Teacher's Day we learn to glorify all the teachers in the world who have contributed in nurturing our souls. I personally feel the mother is the first ever teacher to the child. She teaches the child the importance of appropriate living by the way that she lives her months while she is carrying the little one in her womb. Her attempts are to nurture the growing fetus within with the best of food, drinks, thoughts, feelings and actions. After the birth of the child it is predominantly the mother who teaches the child to brush, to attend to the nature's call, to walk, to talk, to eat, to read, to write and further to develop important values in life – along with the father, and in some cases even the grandparents.

Eventually as parents and teachers, we must realize that there is an immense wealth in each and every child. It is about connecting to the greatness in each child and accepting and celebrating the child as he is. It is not a technique but a 'Way of life.' It is about loving and celebrating the child as he is and not what we wish he was. It is about unconditionally loving the child from our core.

We have to create "AHA" moments for the child by appreciating him or her in every opportunity that we get. Each one of us has both negative seeds (anger, fear, hatred, shame, rebellion) and wholesome seeds of love, joy, compassion, growth. What will blossom depends on the seeds we choose to water and nurture constantly. Greatness is a choice and our children will eventually choose greatness for themselves if we as parents choose to kindle the right seeds within them from the right age. We can do so by giving enough time and attention to what is right.

We all are made in the image of God so how can we be anything but God-like in our very nature? Let us all take the pledge as teachers on this auspicious month of September to emulate and tread the path shown by our great legendary teacher Dr. S. Radhakrishnan. Let us be instrumental in being worthy role models for our children.

Happy Teacher's day!

17

Impossible Today, Possible Tomorrow

Wishing all my young friends a very Happy Navratri, Shubha Vijaya and a festival filled with light. Let the festive season dispel the darkness of ignorance from within. October is the month of festivals starting from 'Navratri' which is a time for hope and prayers, for song and dance, for fasting and celebrating the great Mother Goddess who blesses us in innumerable ways!

Within us there live so many 'asuras' or demons like anger, greed, hurt and jealousy. It is only when we welcome the Great Devi in our hearts can vanquish the darkness within. The tenth day is known as 'Vijaya Dashami' which symbolizes the triumph of good over evil. The name 'Vijaya' signifies 'victory' and 'Dashami' is the 'tenth day' of the Hindu calendar. This particular day is celebrated all over India, with each state bringing its own unique flavor to it. The day marks an important beginning for the year in terms of education, starting a new profession, learning an art form and so on.

15th October, 1931 marks the birth anniversary of APJ Abdul Kalam. Popularly known as the 'Missile Man', he was born in Tamil Nadu to father Jainulabdeen and mother Ashiamma. He was a scientist and the first bachelor to have become the 11th President of India. Words will fall short to describe what he meant to the youth of the nation, being nominated as MTV youth icon in 2003 and 2006. As a scientist he had developed projects PSLV and SLV and developed missiles AGNI and PRITHVI. A recipient of PADMA Bhushan and PADMA Vibhushan, Dr. Kalam was the third President to have received the Bharat Ratna Award before becoming the President of India.

One of the distinguishing qualities that made Dr. APJ Kalam stand out was his simple and humble behavior, his hard work and perseverance which took him from the fishing hamlets of Rameshwaram to becoming the President of India. Despite his humble beginnings he reached his pinnacle of growth as a renowned scientist and the most loved President. There was never a trace of pride or arrogance in him. He extended his 'heart and hand' to help one and all and this made the youth admire him. He always had inspiring messages for youngsters and encouraged them to tap their inner potential which would make each one of them "UNIQUE". He would emphasize on these four tools for building a UNIQUE personality:

* There must be an AIM in life,
* We should continuously acquire knowledge,
* Work hard and
* Persevere to defeat the problem, succeed and eventually realize the aim.

He reiterated the fundamentals for becoming a UNIQUE YOU is 'KNOWLEDGE' and the equation for Knowledge is:

KNOWLEDGE = CREATIVITY + RIGHTEOUSNESS + COURAGE.

One of the main characteristics of 'scientists' is that they never say impossible, because what is impossible today is possible tomorrow. If we dissect 'impossible' we get I AM POSSIBLE. Everything is possible for us when we align ourselves to the belief that nothing is impossible. As Revered Mahatria Ra says:

"The beliefs we hold in the beginning of the journey defines the journey."

When we sit in the car, we know where we have to go and we drive in order to reach there. Similarly, whatever we focus on, that is where our energy goes and eventually we reach our goals. What we think in the beginning defines the result. If we tune our minds into thinking that it is impossible, it will indeed be impossible. While if we attune ourselves with the positive thought – 'it is possible', we will see that all our energies are directed towards achieving what we have set in our minds.

What we require is to develop and cultivate our mind towards positive thoughts and actions. Parents, teachers and the environment play a very important role in shaping the minds of children. All children are alike: very fragile and tender. We cannot say that this child is more intelligent than the other. What we impart to the child makes him different from the others. It is upon us as adults to shape and groom them.

We have enough role models in the world whose footsteps we can follow... But my question is, can we become those parents whose footsteps our children can confidently follow? I feel when we become a parent we shoulder a huge responsibility of nurturing our children. If we, as parents, groom our children with the right moral and ethical values, will we not contribute in creating a better world? Why at all complain that the world we live in, is not safe, is not good? My question is, what are we as parents doing to create a better world? Can we not take the individual responsibility of 'creating our own children?' This itself will add to a better world. Just like droplets of water become an ocean, similarly, each parent can create a child, thus, creating a community of aspiring morally right children.

Adding to this, we should never see the responsibility of parenting as one of burden, but rather of love and care. With love everything is possible. Even the 'impossible' becomes 'possible.' The only thing we require is FAITH in our own selves which will empower us to create the FAITH in our children by showering them with Love, empowering them with good education and enriching them to becoming confident and compassionate individuals who can thus feel with the feelings of others. It could be "Strict Love" at times but it has to be 'Love' at all times.

Mahatma Gandhi and Mother Teresa were propagators of love. The former came to be known as 'The Father of the Nation' who freed India from British Rule through his approach of Non-Violence. We celebrate his birthday on the 2nd of October. It is declared as the 'International Day of Non-Violence' by the United Nations General Assembly to disseminate the message of non-violence through education and public awareness.

Mother Teresa was able to spread love in the hearts of the poor and the needy by further establishing the Missionaries of Charity. She was canonized on the 5th of September, 2016, for the greatest service which one could do for mankind.

This month is filled with festivity and the birth anniversaries of two Great 'Maha-atmas' or "Great-Souls." A message for my young children; *"Let us be inspired by the paths taken by great people, define our own path for ourselves, and follow it fearlessly with indomitable courage."*

A message for the parents, teachers and adults:

Let us be instrumental in creating such children who can feel with the pain and sorrows of others as their own. Through this, we will achieve what God has sent us for. Let's conclude with a poem by William Blake:

"Can I see another's woe?
And not be in sorrow too?
Can I see another's grief,
And not seek for kind relief?
Can I see a falling tear?
And not feel for my sorrow's share?"

18

Be Sensitive to others' Feelings

My dear children, define what you are made of, "Muscles of iron and nerves of steel" as Swami Vivekananda proclaimed. Look up to yourself and never look down. Your potential is as vast as the limitless sky. We are defined and confined by our own thoughts.

India is a nation vast in its cultural heritage and philosophy. What India has contributed to the world is immense. We cannot help but feel proud of our country and strive to give back to her much more than what we have received. We have had great leaders who have shown us the way to rightful living through the way they have lived their lives. We have to learn from them and live our lives in such a way that we are useful to all those around us. As Revered Mahatria says, *"Even a bull is able to look after a family of four. So, can we not as humans expand our mental bandwidth and look beyond me, mine and myself?"*

I would like to reflect upon the life of Swami Vivekananda here to further explain what I write. Parents play an extremely important role in the life of a child. Swami Vivekananda's mother posed a small test for him when he was about to leave for the United States. He would be travelling to Chicago to represent India for his first address on Hinduism in a foreign land. She wanted to be sure if she had been successful in imparting certain core values to her son. One of the most important value being *"To be sensitive to the feelings of others and to never hurt anyone in thought, word and action."*

She asked him to pass the knife to her. The way Swamiji offered the knife to his mother after cutting fruits for himself assured her that he would always take care of others. My dear children, while offering the knife, Swamiji was very careful. He held the sharp edge of the knife towards himself and offered the wooden handle to his mother.

Children have an inquisitive mind and they never tire from asking questions. The more they ask questions, the more they grow in their thoughts, confidence level and approach towards life. Dr. APJ Kalam always encouraged children and youth to ask questions... He believed that a questioning mind has an unquenchable thirst for knowledge. It arises out of sheer innocence from young children and through this internal quest a lot is revealed to them. He always believed that children are the future of the nation.

As Revered Mahatria says, *"We require enough role models whom our children can emulate. As parents and as adults we have to strive towards being a WORTHY ROLE MODEL for them. We have to strive, work hard and be truthful, thus, paving a path which can be easily tread by our little ones."*

The scriptures of ancient India have crafted a wonderful world for us to step into and learn from. Introducing children to these scriptures from a young age would help them to feel one with the past, before they can think of creating a legendary future for themselves. It would give them a mental view of life and people as depicted through the various characters in stories. Above all, introducing children to the mother of all languages Sanskrit would enhance their pronunciation skills and diction from a very young age. All the great saints and leaders of India have emphasized on the learning of Sanskrit. They feel that Sanskrit flows through the blood of every Indian. Every child born in India should know it, just as every child born in France has to know French.

"Sanskrit creates beneficial vibrations of the 'nadis' and strengthens the nervous system contributing to our health magnanimously."

Let us be instrumental in creating CHILDREN who are "Everyone's Future." Let us as parents introduce them to our ancient scriptures and Sanskrit along with school education from a young age to develop important moral, ethical and core values of life in them.

In a way, we are the architects of the future of the world, aren't we?

19

Be a Lesson in Leadership to Your Children

My dearchildren, as we come to the close of yet another beautiful year, let us assign certain benchmarks towards our overall development for the next year. We should aspire to set such standards in our life where we can see an upward spiral of continuous sustained growth. It has to be a life of 'This and That' as Revered Mahatria reiterates. We have to aim to give our BEST towards academics as well as excel in a passion which drives us.

For each one of us, the entire year is generally filled with many events but what we require to do is to learn and improvise from our experiences during these events. To explain in simple terms, the difference between an event and an experience:

Event is the gap between two time intervals. Experience is the response which we exhibit during these intervals.

Hence, experience is a personal phenomenon and it varies from one to the other. Children generally understand and imitate the way parents or elders act. These experiences for children are of paramount importance. We, as adults, should demonstrate it to the best of our capacity through our behavior and actions.

We have to lead them and show them the way to live happily and peacefully with the right moral and ethical values. We pass down traits to our children through heredity and through the environment they grow up in. Both of these influences come from the parents alone. Thus, it is imperative for parents to lead by positive examples enabling the children to be emotionally strong.

Children don't do what WE TELL THEM TO DO, rather THEY DO WHAT THEY SEE. We have to in all ways "WALK THE TALK" and not just TALK. We need to be mindful of our own thoughts, actions and behavior because we are being watched and absorbed by our children at all times. In the way we respond to stress, anger or handle an unfavorable situation, we create a valuable learning experience for our children. Our actions, beliefs and attitudes become integrated into our children's way of being.

My earnest request to all the parents here is to be careful about the behavior we exhibit while we are with our children. God has bestowed us with the wonderful opportunity to help our children become great individuals and moreover, world class leaders. Greatness comes from within and we have to show them that each one is capable of becoming great. I love the way Revered Mahatria puts it:

"LEADERSHIP IS HOW YOU FEEL WHEN YOU ARE ALONE..."

We, as parents and educators, have to believe that they deserve to be leaders in their own ways. Above all, we have to help the children to believe in themselves that they WILL surely LEAD. To conclude, here's a beautiful reference from what the Revered Mahatria says, *"When life throws a dagger at you, there are two ways to catch it. One is by the handle and the other is by the blade."*

We have to teach our children to catch it by the handle and fight their way through. For if they catch it by the blade they will surely hurt themselves. These lessons are very important in paving their way to a successful future. What really matters is what we leave 'in' our children and not what we leave 'for' them.

I wish a very Happy New Year and a Merry Christmas to all my young readers.

Let us revive and recreate ourselves, once again!

20

From Just a 'Be' to 'Being'

I wish a very Happy New Year to my dear young friends! As we have entered into 2017 let us commit ourselves to start with a new beginning and drop off all the baggage we have from our previous year. In our lives, how we look at a situation depends entirely on our state of mind. All the gibberish that we are carrying inside our heads is not interested in us, we are interested in it and are actually creating issues for ourselves by keeping it within. The moment we lose interest in it, and understand the futility of it, it starts disappearing from us.

One very important aspect in 'being' with children is to 'be' like them.

If we break up the word 'being' what do we get?

'Be' – whenever we add 'ing' to any word, it means it is in the state of present continuous, "being'".

So, whenever we say 'being' with somebody and in this case with children, I mean to be with them in the present continuous with all our senses. Our body, mind and soul have to be with them, only then can we 'be' like them. Children, by nature are very spontaneous, always bursting with energy, and are playful.

Playfulness is one of the most essential ingredients in our relationship with children. I feel children respond best while they are playing. Bringing in playfulness, laughter, song, dance, colour, fun, imagination and fantasy together, makes them come alive and increases their receptivity to learning as well.

Subtly through play we can incorporate a learning which we want our child to imbibe. We can see the enthusiasm with which he/she works and makes sure all the others in the environment also comply with them. No one strategy works forever with children. We have to keep changing it to make learning come alive for our little ones. There is a famous saying by Albert Einstein, *"Insanity Is Doing the Same Thing Over and Over Again and Expecting Different Results."*

So, as parents and elders, we have to keep innovating, discovering and imagining whenever we are with children. 'Do something different' is a simple solution but we are at times too lazy to try this. We get stuck with our old habits and patterns which we do not want to break and set ourselves free from. Children learn a lot from simply observing what we do and what we don't.

Let us try to be childlike in whatever we do - playful, energetic, vibrant and above all joyful. I think it is the most exuberant state to be in.

Let's conclude with what Revered Mahatria says, "We are just a distance away from Greatness. Let us go the extra mile... Always surpassing and surprising OURSELVES."

I am ready. Are you?

21

Of Love

Wishing my dear children and parents a very happy Valentine's day!

As a child I used to ask myself, what is the purpose of having one day as a day of love – is not every day a day of love? As I gained maturity, I got clarity from the experiences of life: Every day is a day of love, however, by creating these special days we are able to celebrate, cherish and express our love in a more tangible way.

Sometimes when it is in the context of one day it becomes easy for us to say all that we wish to. I urge all my dear readers to use this Valentine's Day to celebrate love like never before... be it through cards or gifts, through speaking or Silence, through hugs or pats, please let all the people you love know how much you mean to them. Life is too short to keep it all within.

Love for me means many things. It certainly is not limited to what a man or woman feel for each other. Love is what I feel for my family, my dear friends, my work, nature and for my God.

I would love to share a beautiful expression of my love for Him which flowed as a poem and shows various different emotions of love.

Dancing to me
Is my sadhana,
A prayer to my Divine
It takes me to another
World where no one exists,
But me and my God.

O how I love this
Divine Communion
Where at one moment
He pulls my hair,
He teases me and
Stealthily blindfolds my eyes.

Yet in the next moment
I lose myself in His Embrace,
He is my Krishna
My peacock feathered
Blue coloured eternal
Companion and Beloved.

I dance and keep dancing
Emoting my emotions,
Gradually moving away
Into the unknown
With one hand down,
And the other hand up.

The Sufi whirls
So mesmerizing
So Divine
Connecting the mortal
To the immortal
Dissolving all imperfections.

Keeps going endlessly,
Detaching the thread
Of attachment from the transient,
To the Source.
My **Eternal Dance** of Life
In Divine Communion!

Let us keep growing in love, for love is all that really matters.

22

Discover the Formless Presence of God

My dear parents, I would like to quote a few lines from Kahlil Gibran:

"Your children are not your children.
They come through you, but not from you.
You can give them your love, but not your thoughts,
For they come from a land that you cannot enter,
Not even in your wildest dreams."

Kahlil Gibran was an accomplished artist and poet. He is primarily known for his book, The Prophet, a compilation of philosophical essays written in poetic English prose. My reason for quoting a few of his lines here is to bring an awareness for parents that children are unique and we, as parents, should never feel that we are their sole owners. I would like to describe my understanding of each sentence in depth.

"Your children are not your children."

In reality our children are not our children. They have come with their own unique destiny. As Revered Mahatria says, *"Human life takes place only when the formless presence intervenes."* The formless presence intervenes with a purpose destined for each new life. We as parents do not have the right to define and confine that. THE FORMLESS PRESENCE, that is God, is the coauthor of their destiny. Why do we get so attached to our children and thus restrict their growth? This is a question we all should ask ourselves. Professor Dr. A.P.J Abdul Kalam reiterated,

"Have wings to fly. Discover your own potential."

"They come through you, but not from you."

We are the bearers of children as planned and conceived by God, yet they do not come from us. They are in reality God's children and we are only the transient bearers of these souls. So why at all be obsessed about them? I feel what we as parents need to do is impart important values to our children along with good education and a compassionate, kind heart. The rest will be taken care of. If we sow the right seeds with the appropriate manure they will surely sprout into fruit bearing plants.

"You can give them your love, but not your thoughts."

Children require our love, care and time. Very often, as parents, we do not give them our love and care, and most importantly, our time. In the present day scenario, we fill the lives of children with all the toys and gadgets available in the market equating it with the love we have for them. However, I am sorry to say, this is not what they require. Have we ever thought what the prerequisites of growing a seed into a plant are? First and foremost, we require to nurture and take care of it regularly by giving it our time and love. This will ensure that it grows into a plant, removing the weeds from it, as it comes.

Children are as fragile as a plant which without adequate nurturing will die. Sometimes we, as parents, do not realize that we are killing the individualistic dreams and ambitions of our children by imposing our thoughts on them. Let us pledge to give them our love, not our thoughts, and remove from them the weeds of doubt, fear and anxiety as and when it appears.

"For they come from a land that you cannot enter."

We cannot ever fathom what is destined for a child. We simply have to be an inspirational role model for them to emulate. It is futile to merely preach transformation. Let us be that catalyst for transformation and keep inspiring them to aspire because the fact is, what they are destined to become cannot be revealed now, only time will unfold.

We all are born with a divine fire within us. Our efforts as parents should be to channelize this fire in our children towards the right path and direction. Our life will serve its purpose only when we as parents are able to help in the growth of our children, not by possessing them but by liberating them...

I wanted to reiterate these few lines in depth particularly in the month of March when the children are giving their final or board exams. It is imperative for parents to understand this and augment the growth of their children.

My dear children, a small message for all of you from my beloved Mahatria, *"The beliefs you hold in the beginning of the journey defines the journey."* Believe in yourself, that you are not made for ordinary things in life, and you will be the ruling star wherever you go always shining bright and bringing light to the world. Let every cell within you vibrate with Professor Dr. APJ Abdul Kalam's words,

"If you want to leave your footprints on the sands of time, do not drag your feet. Stamp on them!"

Best of luck. For your exams. And more importantly, for your life.

23

"I Can" – Two Words that Drive Positivity

My dear parents and young friends, with the onset of the summer months, let us try to refresh our minds like we do to our bodies with new thoughts and ideas giving our hundred percent to every activity that we do. When we learn to be attentive to our thoughts, words and actions we become mindful and feel energized all the time. This new zeal to live life fills us with a freshness which keeps challenging us to go beyond our own comfort zone.

Dear friends, we have to believe in the potential of "I can." Whenever we tune our minds to "I can", the mind gets programmed in that direction. Parents play a very important role in making the child believe from a young age, "Yes, I can." This builds their confidence as they keep growing up.

I feel what children require is an acknowledgement of what they are doing. Children like to be noticed when they are trying. Once they get the confidence from a very young age about their parent recognizing what they are doing, the self-esteem develops. They start feeling that they can do everything. Conversely, as soon as they feel they are being ignored they give up trying.

As parents, we have to recognize the smallest steps they take, actively involving ourselves in what they think, do and say. It is about listening to our children without passing judgments, jumping to conclusions and attempting to fix their life. In fact, in our desire to fix their life, many a times we end up messing their lives especially when we are unsure about it ourselves.

In the present day scenario children are very sure as to what they want right from a very young age. No longer do parents have to make the choice for two-and-a-half-year-old children as to what they want to wear or eat and also which place they want to visit. They are able to make independent choices very confidently. In fact, the beauty lies when we encourage them to make these choices and let them actively participate in certain choices of ours. Children thrive when they feel they are being appreciated, recognized and valued as human beings.

I feel this is not only true for children but also for adults. It is a very natural human trait to seek for approval and praise in every aspect, whether small or big. Have we ever observed or introspected that when we appreciate our cook for cooking well, the next time he cooks even better? If this is applicable for adults, then why can we not do this consciously while interacting with our children?

The beauty of doing this long enough is that once the self-confidence and self-esteem is built from a very young age, they do not seek for approval as they grow into adults. They learn to undertake projects and deliver them with commitment, leaving the results to the cosmic potent force. As such the entire universe conspires for them. Whatever they do with the purest intention, the cosmic energy blesses them with abundance in some form or the other.

The human mind is programmed towards recognition and praise. So what is recognition? Recognition is about nourishing the heart and soul. Children are tender buds growing in our life garden. In a garden, there are seeds as well as weeds. When we fill the garden with seeds, the weeds go unnoticed. If we fill the child with positive seeds of love, joy and compassion then where is the question of the negative seeds (or call it weeds) of anger, fear, hate and shame to sprout?

In reality, children are the purest and most innocent form of God's creation. After birth, it is we as adults who unknowingly sow into them negative seeds. Let's try to be more careful and cautious as to how we do it. It is by the way we think, act and talk to our children? What will blossom, depends entirely on the seeds we choose to water and nurture.

As children grow up, it is more important to realize that more than WHAT we talk to them, we need to understand HOW we talk ABOUT them. This has a very strong bearing in the minds of our young ones. In my own experience I have seen how my nineteen-year-old son reminds me not to talk 'about' him with others.

Greatness is a choice and our children will eventually choose greatness for themselves if we, as parents, act as the catalyst for them. There is immense inner wealth in each and every child. It is about connecting to this incredible potential in each child and accepting and celebrating the child as he is. In the truest sense it is not a one-time act but a 'way of life.' It is about loving and celebrating the child as he is, rather than constantly lamenting on what he is not.

Parenting is all about unconditionally loving the child from the very core. It definitely requires a major paradigm shift where we as parents and adults start valuing the worthiness of the child as he or she 'IS' rather than enforcing what we want them to 'BE'. For most of our problems there are simple solutions but it is our "brilliant minds" that complicate every simple solution. We have to take a relook at our life.

Each child carries a rainbow. We are like prisms that have to catch their light and bring their unique rainbow into life.We have to connect to the child. This is the major essence of parenting. What do we mean by 'connect?' Connection comes from the heart and not from the mind. It is like the invisible cord from our heart to the child's. Our role as parents is to do whatever we can to pump in radiant light, positive energy, love and joy into the cord.

Feeling excited to play my part – in my son's life, and in that of so many more children. They deserve the best.

24

Revive the Reading Habit

My dear children and parents, I welcome you to a wonderful holiday season. The scorching heat of the summers will encourage parents to spend some quality time with their children within their home, I am sure!

Reading with the children and for the children (when they are still very young and unable to read) is one of the best ways to preoccupy their time at home. Apart from that a lot can be done to tap the child's creativity. Each one of us is very creative, and to the extent that we harness it, it shows up in the world outside. Children learn a lot (unconsciously) from their parents and grandparents; engaging them with a few chores at home enables them to be independent. Simple work like filling water in vessels, kneading the flour and other such small jobs in the kitchen, accompanying the grandparents to the grocery store, keeping an account of the money paid and received are all important life learnings by themselves.

As parents we should enjoy and cherish the time when our children are with us. Every age is special and reveals something beautiful about the child – and ourselves.

The scorching sun seems to be beating down upon the world as if it is punishing it for being reckless with the resources. Every time we step out, it seems we are going to dissolve into a puddle of sweat. So why not make the best out of these summer months and learn, dwell and create … a great suggestion would be to learn about India, the country which offers us our roots.

India, being a land of rich heritage and culture, is blessed with many saints and revered people who have contributed a lot to the world. In this age of distraction children keep observing the elders in the families who are the victims of innumerable gadgets. As Revered Mahatria says,

"Children learn much more from what they see than what they hear."

So, subconsciously they form memory cells of these gadgets used by their parents and slowly start getting drawn towards them. I feel it is primarily the parents' responsibility to wean themselves off, from these addictions so that they can be worthy examples and role models.

I do understand that with the onset of the modern era and advancements in technology, it is imperative to be able touse these devices but we should be aware where to draw the line. Especially when children are around us we should refrain from using these as much as possible – as they are watching and learning all the time.

To reinstate on a poem, A Psalm of Life, "Lives of all great men remind us, We can make our lives sublime, And, Departing, leave behind us, Footprints on the sands of time."

To achieve this, we have to develop the ability to stay away from distractions. The lives of successful people have not been one devoid of hardships or difficulties, yet they survived the test of time with their hard work, determination, courage and faith in self, in others and above all GOD. I feel the ability to effectively deal with distractions and focus on the goal has been an important trait of successful people. Even a child with average capability can succeed if he knows how to stay focused and keep away from distractions. Unfortunately, the opposite too is true. Even a child of extraordinary capability can end up leading a very average life – if they don't stay focused.

I attempt to, in simple words, explain the meaning of the word, 'distraction': "When our attention gets diverted from the activity which we want to do, we get distracted." In the words of Steve Jobs, "Focus is the ability to say 'YES' to the one that is most important to us and 'NO' to the hundred that can be dealt later."

My dear children, let us develop an inexhaustible spirit to work and study. When we study or work there will be problems, but we should never allow problems to become our master. We have to become the master of the problems and SUCCEED. The key to success as students is to study with passion and sincerity. These have its own rewards, which cannot be measured immediately, but its fragrance will keep inspiring each one of you to aspire.

Let's aim to leave our footprints in the sands of time, should we?

25

Parenting is a Specialized Art

My dear parents and children, I welcome all of you back to the fun filled academic year with immense learning happening in every dimension. I am sure there must have been cherished moments of bonding together at home and while travelling as a family.

Many a times when I sit down and contemplate, I feel enamored by the design and chemistry of this human body and human existence. Everything has been planned so meticulously by God, in our bodies and outside our bodies, to enable us to function at our BEST.

I feel nothing in the world comes close to changing us as a person, as much as working with children does. With each of my endeavor in penning down the Editor's Note for children, I feel something at the very core of my being blossoms.

I have learnt a lot from children and I feel parenting has brought about the most intense emotions in me while bringing up my own child. The dominant emotions have been ones of immense joy, gratitude and love.

I feel it is not about them (children), it is about us. Parenting is not about the techniques but our philosophy of life in general. In reality it is not about our children but about us becoming more aware, mindful, sensitive and conscious human beings. It is also about the life lessons we learn on the way that go on to become the most precious gift from our children to us. In that sense, I truly feel – parenting can actually be equated to meditating.

As parents, we have to follow the principle to work on ourselves first. Whatever issues we might be facing with the child, the question is not what our child needs to do, but what we need to realize as a parent first. When we introspect and connect with our child (who has come through us), we shall be able to answer all the queries with ease. For instance, if our child is shy then rather than pushing her to speak up in a social situation, we should ask ourselvesas to why we feel uncomfortable with her shyness and whether it is our need or hers to be socially confident?

So parenting is not about them alone, it is also about us. It is our opportunity for mental, emotional and spiritual awakening. At the core of parenting, or as a matter of fact in any other relationship, there has to be acceptance—A love for what 'IS', rather than struggling and fighting for what 'ISN'T'. No matter how hard we try, can we make a cat bark or an oak sapling grow into a banyan tree? Similarly, parenting taps into our inner beauty and is a joyous responsibility which God has given to a chosen few. Rather than resisting and fighting it, let us accept it gratefully and respond with the best of inner abilities.

Children have infinite potential within them and the way we can tap these will make them SPARK in life... I feel all of us as human beings have an indomitable spirit and strength which we are often unaware of. The more we tap into these by sitting in Silence for a few minutes every-day, or simply closing our eyes and withdrawing ourselves, the more beautiful life will keep becoming.

It is easy to identify what the child does not do, but how often have we appreciated our child when he does something which deserves recognition. This may not be something noteworthy according to the adult, but for the child when the parent acknowledges this with positive comments, he starts feeling that the act was indeed significant. For the child we are his walking, talking, living role models. They will simply observe our behavior and actions and try to replicate it in their lives.

Haven't you seen this in your own life? A girl child of three/four years imitates her mother by dressing like her and a boy child tries to imitate his father by behaving and dressing like him. This trait or attribute continues during the growing years too. We have to be very careful as to what, how, why, when, where we communicate with our child.

Parenting is one of the most beautiful gifts bestowed by God. Let's cherish it to the hilt!

26

Develop the Art of Being Aware

My dear children, it is with the grace of our thoughts, words and actions that we can transform even the deepest of hurt that has been caused to us. In this way, we even let go of our fears and resentments so that we do not harbor negativity and hatred within us. Let us learn to pray for and forgive those who have been unkind to us. A well-directed mind will do us greater service than a mind that is a minefield of negative emotions. When the mind is trained to be focused and positive, it gets gradually disciplined and is able to achieve great heights.

As parents, we play a very important role in guiding our children towards developing 'awareness'. The question arises on how it should be done. Children between two and six years have a mind which can absorb anything and everything. To the extent we expose them to the right stimuli; they will be able to imbibe them. In the current scenario adults themselves are distracted with a plethora of technical gadgets around them and are hence unable to guide or help their children. With this, slowly the ability to be fully aware of the present and for the present situation fades away.

I would like to narrate a small story to explain what I mean by 'being aware of' and 'in the present situation'.

There was a blacksmith in the kingdom of an opulent king. Once, the king decided to pass through his kingdom to oversee the functions of his state. A king is never alone and always has subjects around him. As he was passing by, all the shopkeepers stopped their work and got up to greet him, except for a blacksmith. The blacksmith was so engrossed in his work that he had not noticed the king passing by. This made the king and his subjects very angry. He was asked as to why he had ignored the king! To this the humble blacksmith responded that he had continued sharpening his tools so that he could serve the king better, oblivious of the external surroundings. The sound of the procession did not even register in his ears. It was hard to believe that someone was unable to hear the tumultuous sound of the kettle drums or the uproar of the crowd mixed with constant trumpets of the elephants. There was indeed something special about the blacksmith, and he was duly rewarded by the king for his sincerity in his work.

The learning which we get from this story is that one can develop the art of being aware, of concentrating and being in the present situation no matter who we are or where we are. This is possible only if we are able to make a conscious choice of focusing all our attention on the task at hand. The problem which the parents face is how to develop this in the children.

Believe me parents, the only way to achieve this is by following it ourselves. I truly feel meditation does not mean leaving everything in the real world and creating an illusionary world by retiring to a mountain or a secluded place. Amidst all the chaos and noise in the world, we can learn to take charge of our inner noise through meditation. The art of concentrating all our attention on one thing is meditation (in the most literal sense.)

When we are focusing all our energies on one thing we are able to do it most efficiently and with absolute clarity of mind. Likewise, when we are cooking we should just cook; when we are with our children, we should just be with our children; when we are serving God, we should just serve Him ... there are numerous examples like these from our lives.

The mother is the first teacher for the child. On this teacher's day my sincere request to all the mothers is:

Live your life in such a way that your life itself can be a message to the child. The way you live your life is the way your children will live their lives. So, live it to the hilt, demand most and more from yourselves in every aspect and factor the divine vibrations into whatever you do.

Today as I write, I only write. No wonder I am feeling so meditative.

MOTHER

A word, which defines itself
With unconditional love,
With forgiveness,
With immensity,
Going beyond one's own self,
To only think what more?

Mother is synonymous to
The OCEAN.

Her love as deep as the ocean
The end can never be seen,
Her eyes encompass everything
Yet disclose nothing
But love and love alone.
Can any natural calamity
Ever affect the ocean?
Can any turbulence
Ever shake the love
Which a mother possesses
For her child.

As vast as the sky
Incomprehensible
Unexplainable
Ever calm, ever peaceful,
Nurturing the child within,
Bearing the kicks and pains
Yet ever calm, ever peaceful.

Is what a **MOTHER** means to me!!!

27

Develop the Habit of Dreaming

"When we align ourselves to do God's work, God does our work." As often reiterated by my revered Guru Mahatria Ra, the more and more we do God's work, God does our work. I feel children are the purest of God's creation. Dedicating my life to a cause much larger than me and mine, and aligning myself in the path towards encouraging children to 'Aspire to Inspire' is what my higher purpose is. I strongly believe today's children are the STARS of the future, and as adults and parents what we have to do is kindle that SPARK within them.

With this desire always in my heart, I keep developing myself such to instill moral, ethical and spiritual values in every child whose path crosses mine. Above all, I keep factoring Divine vibrations into my dreams. With my dream to give children a better world to live in and with the grace and blessings of my 'Matha', 'Pitha', 'Guru' and 'Deivam', I have started iSpark, a Holistic Happiness Studio for children in Chennai, India. As Dr. APJ Kalam says, *"Dreams are not what you see in sleep,*

It is the thing which doesn't let you sleep."

While experiencing a very inspiring movie called 'Peaceful Warrior' recently, it was most beautiful to see how the protagonist was unable to sleep, not for any other reason but only because he had a dream to achieve which was much larger than himself. Children too have to develop the habit of dreaming. Many a times we do not realize the power and strength of dreams and we stop pursuing them. All the great exemplary achievers in this universe had the courage to go after their dreams and make them a reality.

While reading an article in the newspaper on daydreaming, it brought a deep insight. Research shows that those who daydream are also very creative and intellectual. It is very important to get a good mentor for our children so why look outside? We, parents can be that mentor helping the children to develop the strength and courage to go after their dreams.

A few things which I personally learnt from my life and can relate it beautifully to the above mentioned movie which I recently experienced:

The people who are the HARDEST to love are the ones who need it the most.

A WARRIOR (in the real sense means a person who can fight his own ego and accept everyone/everything around him with grace) never gives up what he loves and finds his love in what he does.

We should always be conscious of our choices and furthermore be responsible for our actions.

We must keep our sense of humor alive at all times for it gives us great strength which is beyond measure.

I have decided to be a peaceful warrior in this journey of life. You?

28

The Fragrance of Love

"The law of love
Knows no bounds
Of space and time."

— *Mahatma Gandhi.*

To serve with love was his message and Mahatma, as he was called, was able to free India from the clutches of the British with the dagger of 'True love for all'. Quintessentially, we are all connected with the same thread through the same essence. Each one of us is made in the image of God. In His words, *"Love has nothing to do with which country we belong to, or how rich or poor we are, or what religion we follow. Love is like a river. It flows everywhere uniting all."*

Dear young readers, I dedicate this issue to the Father of our Nation, whose life itself was a message for us. He had dedicated his life to the service of others and to a cause which was much larger than himself: A free India through non-violence.

He was doing God's work. God's work is not in serving the idol in a place of worship but to serve the living human race in a way one can best do in their capacity. As Gandhiji aligned himself to doing more and more of God's work, in the way of serving people through love and compassion, God started doing his work. The energy of the cosmos started flowing through him and he was able to gift us with an independent nation after centuries of being ruled.

"With faith, factor divine vibrations in whatever you do," says my beloved guru, Revered Mahatria Ra.

My dear children, today I want each one of you to develop the quality of feeling connected with each other, feeling love emanate from every cell of your body such that LOVE becomes the fragrance of your personality. Wherever you go, spread the fragrance of love.

I would like to narrate a story here:

Once there was a young boy who asked his father about the Supreme power called God. Wanting to explain to the child through actions rather than mere words, the father asked the boy to place a lump of salt in water and leave it. The next day the father asked the boy to remove the salt from the water. The young boy looked into the water but was unable to find the salt. Why was this so? The salt had dissolved in the water. When the father asked the boy to taste the water, the water tasted salty. The father once again asked the boy to check for the salt. The boy gently replied to his father, "I cannot see the salt, father. I only see water which tastes salty." To this the father replied, "None of us can see the Supreme, we can only feel HIM with and within us always. That is the thread which links each one of us and is the essence of this universe."

Let us for once take a pledge in this wonderful month of October when India was blessed with a pure soul like Mahatma Gandhi:

"To make love the fragrance of our personality.

To be able to do everything through this one word called LOVE, leaving behind the lingering fragrance wherever we go."

Love was, love is, love will be... I live my life out of this Truth each day

29

Ordinary Need not Mean Mediocrity

"Do not ask your children
To strive for extraordinary lives.
Such striving may seem admirable,
But it is the way of foolishness.
Help them instead to find the wonder
And the marvel of an ordinary life.
Show them the joy of tasting
Tomatoes, apples and pears.
Show them how to cry
When pets and people die.
Show them the infinite pleasure
In the touch of a hand.
And make the ordinary come alive for them.
The extraordinary will take care of itself.

– *William Martin*

This is a note primarily to the parents as the New Year is approaching and we set certain standards to be achieved by our children. The above quote has great depth related to the children in the present era.

We, as adults and parents, always keep thinking of what more to give to our children materially but this question often lingers in my mind, "Why not think of spending some quality time with them, enriching their lives with values and not just riches?" As I was dwelling on this aspect, the above poem came to my mind and I felt that we have to teach our children to learn to live and enjoy the ordinary moments of life; the extraordinary will take care of itself.

When we talk about 'ordinary', it does not mean mediocrity and certainly does not mean settling for anything less. Rather, it means what we do each day which actually defines our life. A day piled upon a day becomes a week. A week on week, becomes a month. A month on month, becomes a year. And what is life but a compilation of all our years?

Children have an innate ability to wonder. This is one of the most beautiful attributes which allows them to do things without any pre-conceived notions. As adults, we move away from 'wonderment.' So, let us go back once again to discover the child within us, and help the child around us to discover the marvel of life which is in living the everyday, or so called 'ordinary life' with joy and bliss. Joy is in the 'ordinaries' which we make 'extraordinary' by adding a tinge of wonderment to it.

When we pour ourselves into every ordinary activity in our daily life; when we get deeply involved in everything we do; when we make love visible through every action, life starts becoming magical.

Let us keep chanting internally and reminding ourselves that we are a product of the 'extraordinary' creator to marvel upon the 'ordinary' things of life in an 'extraordinary' way.

Can you feel the miracle called life? I sure can...

30

Nurture Individuality in Children

My dear parents, as we herald into the second month of the year, I write this note especially for you.*"Live life afresh with children, your children should do something that you never dared to think of in your life."*

The first thing we should do as parents when God has blessed us with such a Divine privilege is to become a child again, and see life through the eyes of our children. Believe me, it would make life much simpler to stop thrusting our feelings on them. The problem arises when we start fulfilling our unfulfilled desires through our little ones.

Every child has the necessary intelligence to live his life fully. I use the term 'him' for convenience which could imply any gender. We are just an instrument as chosen by God to parent the child. We have to create a conducive environment for him to grow his physical, intellectual and spiritual abilities from a young age. This should start right from the pre-natal stage. It is very important for us as adults to be in touch and aware of our innate feelings. We may not know this - but children are very sensitive to a parent's feeling. If we are happy and make efforts in making the environment happy, we shall contribute in giving the world a HAPPY CHILD. While if we are unhappy and exhibit tension, anger, fear, anxiety and jealousy, we can never expect a child to be free from these negative emotions. So everything depends on us and we should never attribute an external reason for our children for not turning the way we want them to. As Revered Mahatria says, *"My life is my responsibility and no blaming is allowed."*

Children always emulate their parents. The responsibility is primarily ours, that is, 'TO RESPOND WITH ABILITY'. Why blame someone else, especially children, who are made in the image of God – so innocent and pure? We are the co-authors of our destiny, we are responsible to create it or destroy it.

I would say, if we really have the intention of bringing up our children well, we must change our BEING domain. Everything begins from there. We shall be able to magnetize most and more first by being, then by doing, followed by having and finally in the exhilarating feeling of giving.

There is nothing more beautiful than GIVING. As quoted in the famous hymn, "It is in giving that we receive." We shall be able to give, only when we are capable of transforming ourselves. As a parent and being blessed with the privilege of a human birth, we have an incredible responsibility to give back something worthwhile to the world. If we are able to create another being through our parenting especially with love, then we will be instrumental in fulfilling one of the most beautiful responsibilities.

By parenting with love I do not mean to give the child everything he asks for. That is not love, it is mere foolishness. LOVE is to show him that in whichever situation he is put, he will live through it joyously. That is the way we should bring up our children.

It is very important to realize that our children need not do what we did in life. They should be taught to take that daring step to tread into a path unknown and unheard of. Only then will this world progress. We have to be worthy instruments by nurturing young minds and creating LEADERS who can lead the world from darkness to light.

To end with the following prayer of St. Francis of Assisi dedicated to all the young readers. Keeping this prayer in mind, I wish our children will create a new world, through their young, aspiring minds and loving hearts.

"Make me a channel of your peace,
Where there is despair in life,
let me bring hope
Where there is darkness, only light
And where there is sadness, ever JOY."

31

Prayer: A Sincere Missive to God

"If you really want to do something, you will find a way. If you do not, you will find an excuse."

– Jim Rohn

My dear children, the above quote is applicable to each one of us. We must identify what we really want to do and put all our energies into it. Thereafter with faith and commitment we will be able to achieve it.

Faith in God and prayer unto Him are a must for every one for a happy and peaceful life. God has created this world. He is not far away in the sky. He is within us. It is He who has created our parents, our siblings and knows what is good for us. By praying to HIM with an earnest heart we shall be able to lead a good life. Prayer helps us to stay in contact with Him. As Sri Ramakrishna Paramhansa says, *"When we put a post card in a letter box, we surely believe it reaches the destination, so also when we pray to God, it surely reaches His ears."*

Prayer also purifies our mind and takes us nearer to God. It soothes our sorrows and distresses, making our mind receptive and responsive at the same time.

In today's modern world with the advancement of technology, we have moved away from our inner being, which aligns us to prayer. We, as parents, play a very important role in the lives of our children in connecting them with the God within. I feel this to be the sole responsibility of parents. There is a saying, "Show your children Narayan at an early age." Rest will be taken care of. There is no doubt they will blossom into beautiful flowers spreading their fragrance all around them once the core is aligned to God.

As is said in Bhagavad Gita, the Holy Scripture in which the Energy of the Supreme is prevalent, *"Do your duties to the best of the abilities. Before starting a work, at the completion of a task and while inactive. Practice to look upon all creatures as God, mentally bowing down to them; Awaken and perceive that the power of God is with you at all times using you as a mere instrument."*

Apart from this, it is very important to encourage children towards play. For them, play is not just recreation or leisure but an important aspect of growing up. If we wish to understand our children, we must understand his/her play. Through their actions while playing, children express themselves; convey what they cannot express in words. Left to themselves, children will play with anything: empty cardboard boxes will become houses, curtains will become tents, dolls and stuffed animals will talk to each other; kitchen odds and ends will become a drum set! It is not the objects that are as important here as the fantasies that accompany it.

It is indeed fascinating to see a young child playing especially when they are free from instructions. For example, jumping off the sofa again and again: to achieve mastery over something to build a skill and lose the fear of being hurt. Building towers with blocks only to topple them over is yet another way of expressing deep emotions for the child. From aggression to love, from delight to wonder – everything can be seen in a child while he is at play.

When we as a parent actively participate in this free play, the children develop a bond with us. By playing the role well we are making the experience emotionally real for our children and not ruining it for them. Similarly, when the child wants to help in the kitchen or at home, we should encourage the child by letting him/her have a wonderful experience of the same. As children get older, the component of physical play and sports increases and imaginary play tends to decrease. Physical play has an added advantage of creating satisfaction by using the body. It releases aggression and increases the feel good factor – however, as parents I feel we should always keep the element of imagination alive in our children!

I realized something beautiful as I type today – my work is my play too. No wonder it gives me so much bliss and keeps me excited and enthused.

32

Manifestation of the Sub-Conscious Effect

When planning for a year- sow corn.
When planning for a decade – plant trees.
When planning for life – train and educate men.

– Kwan-Tsu

The education of a human being should begin at birth and continue throughout his life. I dedicate this issue to all the MOTHERS who are the first teachers to the child. This month is my special tribute to all the teachers for September 5th (being Dr. Radhakrishnan's birthday). I feel 'education begins before Birth' when the woman is pregnant. To bear a child and see it just as the construction of a body within the mother's belly is not enough. True maternity begins with the conscious creation of a 'being' even as it is within you, by the power of positive thoughts and emotions.

The true domain of a woman is indeed 'spiritual.' We forget this very often. It is extremely interesting to speak to the women of Japan about children. It is their dearest and most sacred subject. Indeed, in no other countries in the world have children taken such an important, such a primordial place. In Japan they are seen as the center of all attention: upon them are concentrated – the hopes of the future.

As a Montessori educator I have interacted with many children and mothers. In one of my interactions, I observed a child who always had a smile on her face. There was an aura around her which drew me to her. In one of the conversations with her mother I understood the reason behind this innate bliss. She had devoted the nine months of her pregnancy, aligning herself to spiritual practices and sitting in Silence on a daily basis.

This was indeed intriguing and I feel compelled to share my own experience. When I had conceived, my father had given me a picture of Lord Krishna as a child. Before going to sleep and as soon as I would wake up, the very first thing I would do is behold the picture. I had kept it at a place where my gaze would unknowingly fall upon it even as I went through my day. I mentally visualized the child looking like that; with curly hair and a gleeful smile on the face. That is exactly how it happened! Since I had seen this picture throughout my pregnancy, the birth of the child was in perfect likeness to this picture. In addition to this, the behavior patterns which he exhibited were also like Krishna.

Pregnancy is indeed a very precious and sacred time in the parents lives – especially so for the mother. It is that glorious period when a woman rises above all ordinary instincts; towards love and spiritual powers. It is the responsibility (to respond with ability) of the mother to *first* focus on her own improvement. Her thoughts have to be always beautiful and pure, her feelings noble, her material surroundings as harmonious as possible; filled with simplicity and humility.

The *second* is to focus upon the child who is developing within. By taking care of her nutrition, her sleep patterns and maintaining high energy levels she is bound to create a child who is a delight, and a matter of pride – not just for her, but for the world too.

This note is my special dedication to all mothers. How true? God could not be everywhere – so he created you and me.

33

Childhood: Forever in Quest of Knowledge

"Children are the hope of the FUTURE and the builders of tomorrow." These words have been quoted and re-quoted many a times from time immemorial. In modern times, efforts are being made to bring up children in the proper way and attempts are being made to give them the right education. But what we fail to understand is the importance of instilling the right values in children from a young age. This is because we often do not comprehend the deeper meaning of the '**CHILD**' as an independent individual.

To be able to understand him we must be aware of his deeper needs. I feel this is where the adult needs to be educated. When we have brought a child into the world it is our primary responsibility to instill in him/her good values and moral ethics. This needs time and commitment. The first thing we need to do is to "become conscious and gain mastery over one's own self so that we never set a bad example for the child." As Revered Mahatria says, *"Children learn much more from what they see, than what they hear."* We have to be living role models for our little ones! It is only through example that education becomes meaningful.

To speak right words and to give advice to a child has very little effect if we do not practice these ourselves. ***Sincerity,***

honesty, straightforwardness, courage, patience, perseverance, peace, calm, self-control are attributes which are much better taught by example than by beautiful speeches. As we consciously practice these qualities, we will see our children reflecting these ideals and spontaneously manifesting them in their behavior.

By nature, children have an absorbent mind and are very sensitive to their environment. We will be surprised by the innumerable questions which keep arising in their minds. We must have the ability to answer them patiently without showing any disturbance. This again is a beautiful trait, which children absorb unconsciously and exhibit in their behavior as they grow up. When our children ask us a question, we should avoid giving an irrelevant answer. Rather we should make ourselves understood in such a way which is accessible to the mind of the listener (who is a young soul still developing his/her mental and physical faculty). I also feel, if we do not know the answer, we should be honest enough to admit to the child and say, "Come on, let us look it up together – either in a book or over the internet!" This develops transparency and a sense of trust in the child.

In the early years of their life, children are unable to understand abstract notions and general ideas. We can train them to comprehend and understand things by using concrete images, symbols or even parables. In fact, a narrative, a story or a parable works better than any number of theoretical explanations. A tale well told stays in the deeper layers of the child's mind, which has the ability to change the way he/she looks at life as they grow up…

Above all, I feel the worst thing to do is to leave our children in the hands of servants/caretakers and try to displace our job to them. Of course, staff can be of great aid – especially in a home where both parents are at work. Yet I personally feel that a parent alone can invest in the making of a child – no other substitute can be good enough.

When children are put in a school they come in contact with a host of new relations. Here again, when we start life with a little more consciousness, they will seek the right company by themselves. The discretion of being able to understand environment and people is transmitted unconsciously in the child in a conducive home. I feel this starts right from the time the mother is pregnant especially till the child is six years of age. It is till the age of six, that the children are at their peak stage of sensitivity!

In conclusion, I would like to reiterate to all parents reading this note 'Parenting a child starts from first parenting/educating ourselves into becoming much more consciously aware of our SELVES."

All of life first begins with the self. I believe this Truth. I am sure you do so too!

34

Perseverance is the Key to Success

"Education is a churning process of regeneration of Man to Human to Divine."

The Dharma (natural duty) of a teacher is to feel responsible for human growth and help the child to cultivate his own virtues. On Children's Day this month, as a mother and teacher, I introspected and once again realigned my teaching methodology from 'what' I will teach to 'how' I would teach. We as adults have to help the children to understand the need to be good, kind, considerate and responsible thus enabling them to discover their talent and potential to the fullest.

Perseverance is certainly the key to success. Right from a young age, children should be taught to respect good health, physical strength and balance. Difficulties and hardships are bound to come along, but staying strong and not giving up would bring out the true winner in each one of us. To be able to endure…our body, mind and soul have to be strengthened and getting this right from an early age is much easier. The later one begins, the more are the efforts required – as prevention is bound to be much easier than cure. The good news, however, is that at any age with dedication and consistency we can always reverse bad habits.

My dear children, you all should aspire for beauty, not merely for the sake of pleasing others or winning their admiration but for the love of beauty itself. Beauty is the ideal which all of us must realize. The human body that undergoes right rituals from a very young age can realize its own harmony and become fit to manifest beauty. We as adults, have to help the child by providing the conducive environment for aiding such growth. Apart from the academic-oriented education given through institutions known as schools, the right physical education should also be focused upon. This should start early in childhood and pursued throughout life.

Just like school education requires much patience and perseverance, physical education too requires dedication and commitment. The education of the body must be rigorous and detailed, far sighted and methodical and should start right from birth. When we start from a young age, it becomes very easy to translate certain important disciplines into good habits as the physical *body is a 'being of habits.'*

As Revered Mahatria says, *"Good Habits have to be cultivated while bad habits grow by itself!"* Seeds have to be sown while weeds grow by themselves. Rather than plucking out the weeds and getting hurt in the process, it is much better to sow as many seeds as possible...

Likewise, if children learn good habits right from the beginning, it will save a good deal of trouble and inconvenience for them and for the others who take care of them. My humble request on Children's Day to all the children is that they pledge to take care of their body which is the only vehicle in this human life helping them to achieve your dreams, aspirations and goals...

My body is my temple. I will give it the respect it deserves.

35

Three Virtues to End the Year

"If the child is left to himself, he will think more and better, if less showily. Let him go and come freely, let him touch real things and combine his impressions for himself."

– Anne Sullivan.

With the advent of the New Year, children are excited to celebrate Christmas and parents are happy to welcome and add another beautiful year in their growing years. The Christmas spirit is all about celebration and cherishing each other – to think of others and to bring the greatest happiness to one another.

Children, by their very presence bring happiness and spread that joy to all those around them, in unimaginable and inexplicable ways energizing the entire environment. The presence of children is quite similar to the sacred chants from any tradition, which also has a positive impact on the environment. Chanting helps us internally and also increases our concentration abilities. Being with children (mind my words: being with children means just *being with children* that is to see, observe and learn from them rather than being in a correcting mode) is the most beautiful feeling when we do not impose our thoughts and decisions on them.

It is the most soul satisfying experience to be with little ones as they spread an unknown happiness in the entire environment with their exuberance and innate curiosity. To be with them, I realize that we have to be 'consciously aware' (our concentration has to be at its peak) as their unending questions, play and tireless energy will urge us to be in the moment, no matter what! Investing time with children is a rare privilege which we as adults are bestowed with.

I want to highlight three important qualities in the growing years to be emphasized upon right from childhood:

* Self-Reliance
* Patience and Perseverance
* Avoiding Wastage

To elaborate on each one of them very briefly:

Self-Reliance Children should learn to enrich their intelligence by concentrating on the task at hand. While mounting on the steps of knowledge they should also be willing to help others when the need arises. Personal effort is extremely important and brings about greater marvels. Children must be encouraged to do their work by themselves as their intellect slowly starts developing by being independent. Since the teaching method in the Montessori environment is not direct teaching and instructed corrections, children learn a lot by observing each other and persevere to do it by themselves without seeking much help. The feeling of accomplishing a task independently fills them with self-confidence which becomes a very important part of their personality.

Patience is a virtue to be developed from a very young age, right from the time they are two years old. The Montessori environment hones the skill of patience very aptly in the child without making use of much instructions. There are single sets of equipment for each learning methodology which teaches the child to wait for their turn. This in turn instills innate patience in them which they are able to realize as they grow up into adults.

One of the very important traits to be considered for the development of children is to show them to take how much is required and **avoid all kinds of wastage...** One thing is certain, that a simple life has never harmed anyone, while the same cannot be said for over indulgence or greed. Citing stories of humble people like Prophet Mohammed shall make the children more aware that devoting one's life to teaching and caring for others, gave him immense pleasure. He led his life for a cause much larger than himself; for the welfare of the society at large.

Let us live and march ahead in 2019 with faith and conviction in ourselves...in God and in the innate potential sleeping within each one of us!!!

Self-Reliance. Patience. And Avoiding wastage – will take us a long way ahead!

DO WE NEED A REASON TO BE HAPPY?

A phrase very often heard!
Do we need a reason to be Happy?

I always say 'Aha! Children',
In the true sense because Children
By their very nature are "Happy!"
Have you ever seen a child "Unhappy?"

Always dancing and swaying,
Thinking what next, what more?
Their mind in a perpetual rhythm
Of play, of movement, of fantasy

I feel the happiest with children,
As it ignites a spark within,
To skip, to dance, to do the craziest
Of things beyond comprehension.

To "whirl like a child,"
Go round and round endlessly
To drop down suddenly
Then jump up again.

The most beautiful of all
Experiences is to keep whirling,
Till the mind says enough
But that enough never happens!

To pause, to stop, to restart.
Is life not the same?
To pause, to stop, to restart,
Like a roller coaster ride.

At other times so fulfilling
In the most silent of expressions
Of a child, a dear one or someone
Unknown yet feels so known.

Happiness is that tool for me,
Which need not make me go
On a high or a crescendo, yet
The inner dance continues...

An acceptance of what is, IS,
And what is not, IS NOT.
This is His Leela,
We are mere puppets in His Hands

Thus playing our part well
For when this act is over,
We all will merge in Him,
Experiencing Bliss and Eternal Bliss!

36

The Spark

"Do not allow your fire to go out, spark by irreplaceable spark. The world you desire can be won. It exists, it is real, it is possible. IT IS YOURS."

– AYN RAND

The new year always looks promising for each one of us. Many new year resolutions are made in January which are forgotten as the year progresses. The above quote by Ayn Rand strikes a note in our minds. It reiterates to us that we should always let the spark within be ignited by our thoughts, words and actions… and sure enough we will be able to achieve anything and everything we desire for. Let us march ahead this year with this wonderful thought churning within… we might just be surprised as to where we reach.

I remember a very thought-provoking story which I want to share here:

In the parlour of an old farmhouse there was an antique grandfathers clock which for more than a hundred and fifty years had never ceased in ticking faithfully. Every morning at day break when the farmer came down, the first thing he would do was to visit the clock to make sure that it was working right. One morning it so happened that as he went into the parlour, the clock began to speak, "For more than a century and a half, I have been working without a stop and perfectly. Now I am tired; don't I deserve to take rest and stop ticking?"

To this the shrewd farmer replied, "Your complaint is unjustified, my good clock! Are you not forgetting that between each tick you have a second's rest!"

After a moment's thought, the clock began to work again as usual.

My dear children, what does this story show you? With a fine balance between work and rest, we can achieve so much. What is important is to never let go of consistency.

The above story aligns itself to the quote of Ayn Rand "Do not allow your fire to go out…" This can only be achieved when regularity and consistency becomes an integral part of us.

"The world is waiting to experience a new YOU, go and live your potential; show to the world what you are made of – ***Muscle of iron, nerve of steel and a mind like thunderbolt***.

Consistency is the key. Keep it close, at all times!

37

Connect with Our Children

My Dear parents and adults, " **More than how we talk to our children, we need to think about how we talk about them.**" We have to think of our children's childhood memories as albums they carry with them for a life. Every day, we are helping them to add different pictures to this album. There might be some pictures which are discoloured, black and white, maybe a little torn or crumpled. Yet as long as they are small and spaced out among the many colourful, vibrant, lively and joyful pictures – this album will nourish them for a lifetime!

Each Child carries a rainbow. We are like prisms that have to catch their light and bring their unique rainbow into LIFE.

Have you ever noticed how children love hearing stories about their early years? They hold on to every word we utter as we tell them about the time they were born, how they cried, how they slept (or didn't), what they liked to eat, their first words, their first steps, their first day at school, lullabies we sang for them, bedtime stories, songs, toys, their antics, quirks, oddities and fancies. All are laid out like a collage of multiple hues in front of their eyes. These are the stories they hold on to that are told and retold to them till they acquire a life of their own.

Let us do this many a times with our young ones as this can fill us with a sense of wonder, humour, warmth and above all CONNECT with our children at the subconscious level. Connect is the essence of parenting. It is the foundation and core of our relationship with our children. This comes from the heart and not the brain. IT is like an invisible cord from our heart to the child's. As parents we have to do whatever we can to keep pumping radiant light, positive energy, love and joy into this chord. Rest will be taken care of.

"FOR OUR CHILDREN, WE ARE THE ONLY KORAN THEY WILL READ IN THEIR LIFETIME; THE ONLY VEDAS THEY WILL SEE; THE ONLY BIBLE THEY WILL EXPERIENCE; THE ONLY DHARMA THEY WILL FOLLOW.

YOUR LIFE AND MY LIFE WILL EITHER SERVE AS A WARNING OR AS AN EXAMPLE. I KNOW IT IS AN AWESOME RESPONSIBILITY BUT HOW ELSE CAN YOU EXPLAIN WHY YOU CAME INTO THIS PLANET BEFORE THEM? "

as quoted by Revered **Mahatria Ra.**

Let us not pressurize our children and burden them with things we have been wanting to do. To excel, do well in studies, be physically fit and active, socialize (and be popular), listen to us, be respectful, be responsible, be independent, be organized, manage their time well, value money, not be angry or rude or scared, be confident, be happy. When we in reality do not exhibit all these qualities yet we expect them to have each one of these and above all develop these as quickly as possible. Let us accept them first as they are! Yet silently through our expressions and not sermons, strive to fill their lives with enough values which they can live by and ourselves be a role model worth emulating in all ways...

Like begets like

In the history of existence, there has never been and there will never be another like you. Each person is unique and the only one of his kind. In the eternity of time and space there has never been and there will never be a duplicate. Each one of us are distinct. Given the same situation, no two human beings react in the same manner. As parents and teachers we have to identify the innate potential of each child and tap it, make it his strength. Try to understand his wiring.

"There is no end to education. It is not that we read a book, pass an examination and finish with education. The entire lifetime is a process of learning from the time we are born to the moment we die. We have to be fearless at every stage of life." As parents we are constantly learning from our children as they are growing up.

There is a saying "Like begets like." What we think, we draw into our lives. Think big and we shall draw abundance in our lives. Think small and we will live a life of mediocrity.

As parents, are we marveling at the sparkling light that they carry with them or get lost in the shadows where the light does not reach? Are we giving enough messages of 'you are worthy as you are' to your child? Or just keep thinking of what he has not? What we ***focus on grows.*** When we think our children will do very well in life despite anything, irrespective of everything, they ***actually do very well.***

My Revered Guru, Mahatria says "The intent of a parent acts as a blessing in the child's lives." We should always harbor good thoughts for our children.

I do not categorise myself as a good or bad parent. I believe parenting is a daily practice, a mindful one that I work on every day. I feel the following poem written by Rabindranath Tagore, should be etched in the minds of children from a very young age. The deeper meaning of which would definitely give the young ones some healthy food for thought during their growing years:

" Where the mind is without fear and the head is held high.
Where knowledge is free,
Where the world has not been broken up into fragments
By narrow domestic walls,
Where tireless striving stretches its arms towards perfection
Where the clear stream of reason has not lost its way
Into the dreary desert sand of dead habit
Where the mind is led forward by THEE
Into ever widening thought and action
Into that heaven of freedom, my Father, let my country awake. "

We should be like the LION, fearless and strong, aspiring to do things which are bigger than our own selves. Nothing should ever pull us down. Our main objective should be to keep on striving and aiming to give our BEST in everything. We should go beyond our independent will into a much larger plan as crafted by HIM. The mind should be liberated from the bondage of self into the world of freedom to keep giving most and more in all aspects...

38

Develop the Art of Questioning

"Young children have the natural ability to express themselves and not worry too much about what others think. They are not tainted by the pressures that develop as they begin to deal with peer pressure and develop a fear of failure. So consequently, they have the tendency to be themselves and feel good about it." Phil Barlow.

Life is constantly throwing questions at us and the more we question, the more we learn!

Dr. APJ Kalam has autographed and written in the emagazine, "***To generate questioning and questioning.***" At the time when he was writing this I wondered why had he written so?

As I look back into the years from when it started in 2014 to now 2019, I get my answer. Working with children for many years in the Montessori environment, teaching Kathak and Yoga and presently at my Holistic Studio, "iSpark" I feel children's mind are a flood gate of questions.

How many questions they carry in their little brain?

How many answers they seek?

With how much innocence they still play around and remain happy while most of their complex questions remain unanswered and unresolved in their head. It is overwhelming to think how much more they have to know and learn not through education alone but from everyday life too...

For us adults too, will education or science ever be able to give us all the answers?

Will all the scriptures, philosophical masters and spiritually evolved souls be able to answer all our questions?

Every question answered leads to a new question. Every maturity gained leads to bigger and better challenges to deal with.

Isn't it a fact that every learned and acquired qualification helps us to know how much we don't know yet?

With every bit of knowledge gained are we not becoming aware of how much more ignorance is there in us, yet to be dispelled?

Every clarity gained is leading us to a new seeking.

I feel parental responsibility is in enabling the children to think through the questions they ask. The world is what it is today because of the questions some people have asked. It is in finding the answers to these questions that we have become what we ought to be. We celebrate and revere those who provide the solutions and answers but I think the real path *breakers and path finders are those who have daringly questioned the obvious and asked the uncommon questions*. They are the ones who have paved the path of the future for themselves and others. From a young age, it is the responsibility of the parent/adult/leader to help the children/young ones/team to find the answers and enable them to ask the right questions at the right time!

Any answer is always preceded by a question and only because of compelling questions breakthrough solutions are born. ***Answers are only the effect, questions are the cause!*** Shouldn't we as adults and parents, then train the mind of our young ones to "*generate questioning and questioning.*" I now realize the reason he had written this profound statement. I too am living life and growing in maturity from each experience life gives me.

In that sense, if life can be called a question? Can we; by the way we live our life be the very answer to our question!

Children should ***ASPIRE TO INSPIRE*** by having an inquisitive mind and developing the art of questioning. There are no right questions or wrong questions. A question is a question when it has come to our conscious awareness. *A question will for sure find its answer.* So why not dare our children to ask questions and trod the untrodden path with Faith, conviction and self-belief. Only with faith and fearlessness, can these players of the future migrate smoothly in the present.

How true when I live life with this FAITH, life gives me the BEST!

Why don't you too?

39

Are We a Threat or An Example?

In the words of my Revered Mahatria, I would like to reiterate, " Your life, my life and the lives of each one of us will either serve as a Warning or as an Example. For our children, we are the only Quran they will read in a lifetime; the only Vedas that they will see; the only Bible they will experience; the only Dhammapada they will imbibe and the only Dharma that they will follow."

How we behave and act is our responsibility to the next generation. In our own little ways let us always be that someone whom the world salutes. It is an awesome responsibility but the most beautiful one I must confess. I was touched with the following story which I would like to share with all my readers (young, old of any kind) here.

Once upon a time not too long ago a farmer, living in the mountainous section of one of the southern states, brought home a new wife to become the stepmother of his two small boys. The wife brought with her two sons of her own, and in due time a fifth son was born of the marriage.

The home was typical of that mountain country, and the farmer was the product of four generations of his people born and reared in poverty and illiteracy.

His wife, however, came from a more prosperous section of the state and had received the benefits of a cultural background and a college education. She was not the type to accept poverty and illiteracy without protest.

The evening on which the farmer brought his new wife to their home he introduced her to relatives and friends who had gathered there for the wedding reception. And finally he introduced her to his eldest son, a lad of nine years, with the following words: "And now I wish you to meet the fellow who is distinguished for being the worst boy in this country and will probably start throwing rocks at you no later than tomorrow morning."

The stepmother went over to the young "Jessie James," placed her hand under his chin, tilted his head upward, looked squarely in the eyes for a moment, and then turned to her husband and said, "You are wrong. This is not the worst boy in the country, but the smartest, who has not yet found the proper outlet for his enthusiasm."

Then and there began a friendship between that young boy and his new mother which was destined to project its influence for good throughout half of the civilized world. That was the first time anyone had ever called the boy smart. His relatives, including his father, as well as the neighbours, had built him up in his own mind as being a bad boy, and he had not disappointed them. His stepmother, in one brief sentence, changed all that!

Think of this story, fathers and mothers, for you have it within your power to influence your youngsters. You may be inspired to work miracles in the lives of some who need only the right influence to give them start on the road that leads to happiness.

The stepmother was a small woman, but what she lacked in size she more than made up in ambition and enthusiasm. She proved to be an example for the family and with her love and empathy was able to win the heart of a young boy and transform him into becoming a role model for others to follow. Each one of us have the power within us to live a life worthy of our own potential. Let us tap it and inspire others to aspire...

40

The Spiritual Embryo

"Children should be regarded as spiritual beings capable of great I mental life, deserving respect and stimulation. It is the responsibility of the adult of how we are able to nurture this in the child from the time of conception."

– Dr. Maria Montessori

I was undergoing a one year Diploma program in The Montessori Method of Education from an Institute in Kolkata in the year 1996. This was an International program affiliated to the London Montessori Centre. All our course materials were from London and periodic assessment papers were sent to different examiners based in London.

As days passed by I felt the course was ***educating me*** instead and I could feel an inner transformation happening.

The one year program was divided into various modules with theory subjects like Child Psychology, Philosophy of Education, The Psychic Being, The Spiritual Embryo and many more related to learning more of human behavior. As Educators for young children it was imperative for us to go into the depth of behavioral psychology to be sensitive towards their feelings and emotions.

A subject very close to my heart was that of 'The Spiritual Embryo.' To understand firstly that human birth is possible only when the presence of God gets established and secondly during these nine months the foetus (in general terms the unborn child) should be nourished with good food for the development of a sound body, mind and soul.

"The soul has its origin in the spiritual worlds of God. It is exalted above matter and the physical world. The individual has his beginning when the soul associates itself with the embryo at the time of conception."

The above words had impacted upon me greatly and my perspective towards pregnancy and child birth changed miraculously. I started internalizing these learnings and felt how important it is for me to take on this responsibility to nurture children with the appropriate environment and upbringing.

As I was going through my studies I deciphered Montessori as a life philosophy to embrace and carry with me through my life time.

And motherhood can never be defined, it is a process and we keep discovering our self and evolving through each discovery...

This article is a salute to all mothers and above all salute to MOTHERHOOD itself. My Deepest Gratitude to God for blessing me with this human birth as a woman to be able to carry another life within me.

In giving love I truly discovered I am nothing but love and all I have to do is keep loving and keep giving...

41

Motivate, Do Not Demotivate

To live content with small means; to seek elegance rather than luxury, and refinement rather than fashion; to be worthy, not respectable, and wealthy not rich; to listen to stars and birds, babes and sages, with open heart; to study hard; to think quietly, act frankly, talk gently, await occasions, hurry never; in a word, to let the spiritual, unbidden and unconscious, grow up through the common - this is my SYMPHONY!

– William Ellery Channing

The above expression by William Ellery Channing has touched me deeply. Each word is a revelation by itself. As we go deeper and deeper in its meaning we shall be able to understand its inner depth.

My Dear Parents, we have to be role models for our children. We have to live simply than ostentatiously, be content with what we have and inspire our children with good thoughts, words and actions.

Motivating children increases their self- esteem.

Every tree was once a plant. A tiny plant, being very sensitive, can get easily destroyed due to heavy rains, hailstorms, droughts, parasites etc. in infancy itself. Whereas, fully grown trees can withstand the fiercest of storms. Children are sensitive in the same way. A plant needs proper attention, while tree is self-dependent. Likewise, it is essential to focus on a child's holistic development. Children need encouragement; if parents cannot motivate them, the least they could do is not demotivate them. After studying rigorously for months, a child gets a score of 80 percent in his exams but, instead of accolades, the first thing that comes out of the parents is: "Who got the highest score and what was it?" The child's morale rapidly plunges, and he starts thinking that he may not be able to achieve anything.

42

Be a Friend First and then a Patron...

It has been said in an ancient Sanskrit literature - 'The son should be pampered till the age of five. Once he turns five, he must be disciplined till the age of ten and after the age of sixteen, the parent must manage to make a friend out of him.'

In this ancient stanza, a simple solution has been provided to an important issue. What do children do? Where do they go? Who are their friends? What mental phase are they going through? Often parents are unaware of all the above. Many children get emotionally distressed during teenage and in many cases, parents do not act until it is too late. As mentioned in the verse, after the completion of 16 years, make a friend out of your son. Why so? When children are going through a tough situation, and if there is no friendship or bonding between them and parents, they are more likely to share their grief and pain with their friends. These friends have similar maturity levels as the boy or girl and would not be able to provide the right solutions.

But if, children have an open relationship with their parents, they will not only be inclined to inform them about every minor detail of their life, but will also take suggestive measures prescribed by the parents. And hence, parents will be able to prevent their children from getting misguided or taking the wrong steps.

This teacher's day on 5 September 2019, let us first strive to use kind positive words while interacting with our children and with all the others in the environment (at least in their presence) since they observe every act of ours. Over and above, the BEST gift we can give them as parents is to become a FRIEND to them. Believe me, we win half the battle in this process! By becoming a friend to them we no longer feel superior to them but acknowledge them as our counter-part, as an independent individual ... who too has the right to think, feel and act ... the start of a new beginning!

43

Families must Evolve

Our financial economy does need a boost so buying and giving material things to children is the nature of our world. But our moral economy needs a much greater boost and there is no better way to turn that around than by giving love and time to children. Just love and time – it costs you nothing yet gives so much.

Today, a disproportionate amount of time is being spent on improving external official relations, and a lot of effort goes into it. But, a man's focus on developing family relationships seems to him as big a task as finding a mustard seed in a heap of grain. Today, a bigger problem than inflation, demonetization and terrorism is the increasing detachment in family relationships. The worst use of time is to do something very well that need not be done at all.

A small boy questioned his father, "Pa, how much do you earn in an hour?" The father was furious at first on hearing such an inappropriate question and strongly condemned the son for the same. At night, once his work for the day was over and he was in a more relaxed frame of mind, he approached his son who lay on his bed and asked- "Son! Why did you ask me such a question this morning?" The son said nothing. The father said "I earn 500 rupees an hour, so tell me what do you want." The child removed some cash from under his pillow and said "Pa, I am 200 rupees short of 500 rupees." The father immediately handed him 200 rupees. The child, "Pa! you said you earn 500 rupees an hour, so take these 500 rupees and give me an hour of your time." On hearing this, the father's eyes filled with tears of guilt and humiliation.

It is a common misconception that investing gives returns in business alone...Are investments in relationships not needed? Are investments in spiritual practices not needed? Are investments in virtues not needed? No doubt that financial investments provide financial profits; it is needed and let us also understand that it is momentary. But investments in relationships can be useful throughout life and investments in spiritual practices and virtues will reap profits even across births.

Above all I strongly feel by investing quality time with our children we are doing our best to nurture young plants into strong trees. We are laying a very strong foundation for their growth with our love and quality time. The family is at the heart of any nation.

If we want our nation to progress, we need our families to evolve. So what are we doing as adults, parents and educators? Let us introspect and seek the answer within. Our consciousness shall guide us and direct us towards the right direction.

People normally count only the floors and unfortunately, don't focus on the foundation beneath the ground since it is not visible. The building actually rests on that well laid out foundation, which gives it, its strength and stability. If we lay down the 'right' constitution for our families, it will strengthen our ties. And stable families are the foundation for a strong nation.

So here we begin…let us Herald into the future to create strong families through our young ones…

I affirm to myself "Wait not, Tarry no more!

Keep marching Keep going with one pointed focus…investing time and love for our children."